MODERN
One-Block
QUILTS

22 Fresh Patchwork Projects

Natalia Bonner *and* Kathleen Whiting

stashBOOKS.
an imprint of C&T Publishing

Text copyright © 2013 by Natalia Bonner and Kathleen Whiting

Photography and Artwork copyright © 2013 by C&T Publishing, Inc.

Publisher: Amy Marson

Creative Director: Gailen Runge

Art Director / Book Designer:
Kristy Zacharias

Editor: Karla Menaugh

Technical Editors: Susan Nelsen and
Alison M. Schmidt

Cover Designers: Kristy Zacharias and
Christina Jaruamay Fox

Production Coordinator: Jenny Davis

Production Editor: Alice Mace Nakanishi

Illustrator: Jessica Jenkins

Photo Assistant: Mary Peyton Peppo

Photography by Nissa Brehmer and
Diane Pedersen of C&T Publishing, Inc.,
unless otherwise noted

Published by Stash Books, an imprint of C&T Publishing, Inc., P.O. Box 1456,
Lafayette, CA 94549

Library of Congress Cataloging-in-Publication Data

Bonner, Natalia, 1982-

 Modern one-block quilts : 22 fresh patchwork projects / Natalia Bonner and
Kathleen Whiting.

    pages cm

 ISBN 978-1-60705-723-9 (soft cover)

 1. Patchwork--Patterns. 2. Quilting--Patterns. I. Whiting, Kathleen, 1959- II. Title.

 TT835.B6265 2013

 746.46'041--dc23

               2013011955

Printed in China

10 9 8 7 6 5 4 3 2 1

Contents

Dedication

This book is dedicated to Emmy and Gage Jasperson, Kathleen's parents and Natalia's grandparents, who at 79 years of age pieced and helped to piece several of the quilts in this book, unpicked quilts, spent hours figuring out patterns, and even repaired sewing machines. Thank you so much for teaching both of us the love of sewing, both art and precision. You are amazing!

Acknowledgments

Special thanks to both our families for supporting us along the journey of writing this book.

To Ashlee Woolf, Ainslee Howells, and Ilene Peterson, thank you for the gorgeous quilts that you pieced for this book.

Emmy and Gage Jasperson, thank you for your support, encouragement, and willingness to sew multiple quilts, unpick quilts, and repair sewing machines.

To everyone who reads our blog and attends quilt guilds with us, your kind comments and support gave us more motivation and encouragement than we could have ever imagined.

Thank you to Moda Fabrics, Riley Blake Designs, Michael Miller Fabrics, Birch Fabrics, Windham Fabrics, Robert Kaufman Fabrics, Warm & Natural batting, and all the brilliant fabric designers. The fabrics that you provided for this book are lovely and helped us to create beautiful quilts.

To all the staff at C&T Publishing and Stash Books—thank you very much for giving us the opportunity to write this book. This journey has been so much fun.

Introduction

WE ARE CRAZY ABOUT QUILTING.

We like the feeling that we are creating something useful as well as adding design to our homes. Displaying color and artistry on a bed enhances the room as well as giving the satisfaction of creating an inviting space.

Making one block and turning it different ways to create a pattern can be fascinating. Today's fabric choices open up even more possibilities for design and depth in both the block and the quilt. It is fun to see what we can create.

We love the way different colors and shapes can be used in decorating to affect our moods and emotions. When it comes to decorating our homes, we can change the feeling of a room with a quick change of a quilt on a bed, draped over a chair or couch, or hanging on a wall. One-block quilts especially lend themselves to create interesting patterns that enhance a room when they are folded across the bed or even over a ladder. The effect can come from the pattern and from the color. Straight lines can create a modern, bold feeling, whereas rounded or curved lines induce a soft, more romantic atmosphere. Reds and oranges can be energizing, blues and grays more calming. Green is considered a neutral and will create a relaxed feeling, while yellow lightens the mood. Purple stirs creativity, while brown adds sophistication.

This book includes 22 blocks that appeal to today's quilters, from the beginner to the more advanced quilter. The blocks range in size from 6″ × 6″ to 12″ × 24″, and instructions are given for baby, throw, and coverlet sizes. The coverlet size is large enough to use on beds of various sizes.

Think of the way design and color impact your emotions, and decide what kind of feeling you are ready to create. Choose the block and fabric colors, and then you are ready to enjoy the process.

Sewing BASICS

The quilts in this book are constructed with many common elements: snowballs, half-square triangles, Flying Geese, and template piecing. The steps in each project show one way to construct the blocks for the quilt. For example, a quilt may have Flying Geese elements within a block, and the steps will explain one method for making Flying Geese. However, there are other methods for constructing Flying Geese, and this section explains some alternative methods for achieving the same elements in a quilt. At the end of this section, you will find basic instructions for finishing a quilt: layering, quilting, and some choices for binding the quilt to add the finishing touches.

Snowball Corners

Refer to the project instructions for the sizes of the squares.

1. Lightly draw a diagonal line from a corner to the opposite corner on the wrong side of a smaller square. Place the small square on the corner of a larger square, lining up the outer edges as shown.

2. Sew on the diagonal line from corner to opposite corner on the smaller square. Repeat on all 4 corners.

3. Trim ¼″ beyond stitching. Press triangles toward the corner.

Stitch.   Trim.   Press.

Half-Square Triangles

Here are two easy methods for making half-square triangles.

No-Waste Method

Refer to the project instructions for the sizes of the squares.

This method starts with squares that are ⅞″ bigger than the desired finished size. It makes 2 blocks at a time. Suppose you want a finished 3″ half-square triangle. Using this method, you would cut 2 squares 3⅞″ × 3⅞″ and follow these steps.

1. With right sides together, pair 2 squares. Lightly draw a diagonal line from a corner to the opposite corner on the wrong side of the top square.

2. Sew a scant ¼″ seam on each side of the line (Figure A).

3. Cut on the drawn line (Figure B).

4. Press open, and trim off dog-ears (Figure C).

Sew.

A.

B.

C.

Refer to the project instructions for the sizes of the squares for this half-square triangle method.

This method starts with squares that are only ½″ bigger than the finished size, so it's perfect for those times when you want to use small scraps or precuts. The downside is that it makes only a single half-square triangle per pair of squares, so there is a little waste. Suppose you want a finished 3″ half-square triangle. You would cut 2 squares 3½″ × 3½″ and follow these steps.

1. With right sides together, pair 2 squares. Lightly draw a diagonal line from a corner to the opposite corner on the wrong side of the top square.

2. Sew along the line.

3. Cut ¼″ from the sewing line.

4. Press open.

Stitch.   Trim.

Press.

Strip Piecing

Strip piecing is a way to sew multiple units quickly. Refer to the project instructions for size information. Cut strips into sections as indicated in the pattern.

For example, if you need 20 units of two-patch blocks, follow these steps:

1. Cut the strips as directed in the pattern.

2. Place the strips right sides together and sew a ¼″ seam along a long side.

3. Press the seam toward the darker fabric.

4. Cut the strips into two-patch sections as directed in the pattern.

Flying Geese

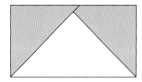

The traditional Flying Geese block is familiar, with its two small triangles sewn on the short sides of a larger triangle. This block can be constructed using several different methods, and here are some methods for you to try. To calculate sizes, remember that a finished Flying Geese block is traditionally a true rectangle, twice as wide as it is tall.

Easy-Sew Method

This method uses a rectangle and 2 squares. Remember that a finished Flying Geese block is twice as wide as it is high. Suppose you want a finished 2½″ × 5″ Flying Geese block. You would cut a rectangle 3″ × 5½″ and 2 squares 3″ × 3″, and follow these steps.

A.

1. Lightly draw a diagonal line from a corner to the opposite corner on the wrong sides of the 2 squares (Figure A).

2. With right sides together, place a square on an end of the rectangle. Sew directly on the line, trim the seam allowance to ¼″, and press open (Figure B).

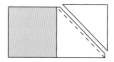

B.

3. With right sides together, place the other square on the other end of the rectangle. Sew directly on the line, trim the seam allowance to ¼″, and press open (Figure C).

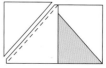

C.

No-Waste Method

This method makes four Flying Geese blocks at a time, using one large fabric square and 4 small fabric squares. Cut the large square 1¼″ larger than the unfinished width of the Flying Geese block. Cut the smaller squares ⅞″ larger than the unfinished height of the Flying Geese block.

> **tip**
>
> For color planning, please note that the small squares become the side triangles in these finished blocks, and the large square becomes the center triangles.
>
> Suppose you want finished 3″ × 6″ Flying Geese. You would cut a square 7¼″ × 7¼″ and 4 squares 3⅞″ × 3⅞″, and follow these steps.

1. Lightly draw a diagonal line from a corner to the opposite corner on the wrong sides of the 4 small squares.

2. Place a small square in opposite corners of the large square, right sides together. The diagonal lines will overlap in the center as shown. Sew a scant ¼″ seam on each side of the line (Figure A).

3. Cut on the drawn line. You now have 2 units (Figure B).

4. Press the small triangles away from the larger triangle (Figure C). (The illustration shows a single unit.)

A.

B.

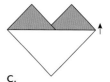

C.

5. On the front side of a unit from Step 4, place a small square on the remaining corner of the large square as shown. Sew a scant ¼″ on each side of the drawn line (Figure D).

6. Cut on the drawn line. You now have 2 units (Figure E).

7. Press the triangles toward the outside to complete 2 Flying Geese blocks. Trim off all the dog-ears (Figure F).

8. Repeat Steps 5–8 to complete 2 more Flying Geese blocks.

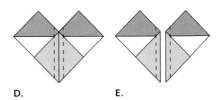

D.   E.

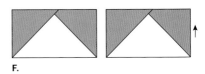

F.

Half-Square Triangle Method

For this method, use completed half-square triangles (page 7) that are ½″ larger than the finished height of the Flying Geese. Suppose you want finished Flying Geese 3″ × 6″. You would use 2 completed 3½″ × 3½″ half-square triangle units and follow these steps.

1. Sew 2 completed half-square triangle units together, matching the fabric at the center seam.

2. Press.

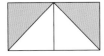

Template Piecing

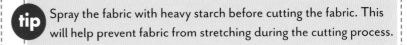

tip Spray the fabric with heavy starch before cutting the fabric. This will help prevent fabric from stretching during the cutting process.

1. Photocopy the patterns at the percentage indicated in each project.

2. Trace the patterns onto template plastic. Mark the template with any markings indicated on the pattern. Cut pieces on the outer line of the pattern.

3. Keeping the templates with the marked side up, place them on the fabric to cut the number of pieces indicated in the project instructions. It's best to cut strips of fabric to fit the template width, and then rotate or slide the template along the fabric strip as you cut.

4. Often on a pattern you will see a letter *r* after the template letter. This means that you will flip the template over to cut the reverse shape of the template. Follow the project instructions for the number of pieces to cut.

5. On the back of each fabric piece, make a small pencil dot at each corner of the sewing lines.

6. When positioning fabric pieces together for sewing, place the top piece right sides together with the bottom piece. Take care to match the intersections of the sewing lines.

7. Stitch along the sewing line. If the pattern has an inset seam, stop stitching and backstitch at the end of each stitching line.

Finishing the Quilt

Backing

Plan on making the backing a minimum of 8″ longer and wider than the quilt top. Piece, if necessary. Trim the selvages before you piece to the desired size.

To economize, piece the back from any leftover quilting fabrics or blocks in your collection.

Batting

The type of batting to use is a personal decision; consult your local quilt shop. Cut batting approximately 8″ longer and wider than the quilt top. Note that your batting choice will affect how much quilting is necessary for the quilt. Check the manufacturer's instructions to see how far apart the quilting lines can be.

Layering

If you are taking your quilt to a longarm quilter, you don't need to layer or baste it.

Spread the backing wrong side up on a large, flat surface and tape the edges down with masking tape. (If you are working on carpet you can use T-pins to secure the backing to the carpet.) Center the batting on top, smoothing out any folds. Place the quilt top right side up on top of the batting and backing, making sure it is centered.

Basting

Basting keeps the quilt "sandwich" layers from shifting while you are quilting.

If you plan to machine quilt on your domestic machine, pin baste the quilt layers together with safety pins placed a minimum of 3″–4″ apart.

Begin pin basting in the center and move toward the edges, first in vertical and then in horizontal rows. Try not to pin directly on the intended quilting lines.

If you plan to hand quilt, baste the layers together with thread using a long needle and light-colored thread. Knot one end of the thread. Using stitches approximately the length of the needle, begin in the center and move out toward the edges in vertical and horizontal rows approximately 4″ apart. Add two diagonal rows of basting.

Quilting

Whether by hand or machine, quilting enhances the pieced or appliquéd design of the quilt. You may choose to stitch in-the-ditch, echo the pieced or appliqué motifs, use patterns from quilting design books and stencils, or do your own free-motion quilting. For more about free-motion quilting, a good guidebook is Natalia's *Beginner's Guide to Free-Motion Quilting* (by C&T Publishing).

Binding

Trim excess batting and backing even with the edges of the quilt top.

DOUBLE-FOLD STRAIGHT-GRAIN BINDING

If you want a ¼″ finished binding, cut the binding strips 2¼″ wide and piece them together with diagonal seams to make a continuous binding strip. Trim the seam allowances to ¼″. Press the seams open.

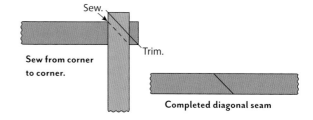

Completed diagonal seam

Fold the strip in half lengthwise with the wrong sides together. With raw edges even, pin the binding to the front edge of the quilt a few inches away from the corner, and leave the first few inches of the binding unattached. Start sewing, using a ¼″ seam allowance.

Refer to the drawings below. Stop ¼″ away from the first corner (Step 1), and backstitch one stitch. Lift the presser foot and needle. Rotate the quilt one-quarter turn. Fold the binding at a right angle so it extends straight above the quilt and the fold forms a 45° angle in the corner (Step 2). Then bring the binding strip down even with the edge of the quilt (Step 3). Begin sewing at the folded edge. Repeat in the same manner at all corners.

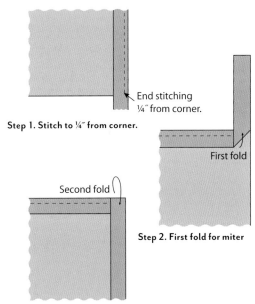

Step 1. Stitch to ¼″ from corner.

End stitching ¼″ from corner.

First fold

Step 2. First fold for miter

Second fold

Step 3. Second fold alignment

Continue stitching until you are back near the beginning of the binding strip. See Finishing the Binding Ends (page 13) for tips on finishing and hiding the raw edges of the ends of the binding.

CONTINUOUS BIAS BINDING

A continuous bias binding involves using a square sliced in half diagonally and then sewing the resulting triangles together so that you continuously cut marked strips to make a single, long bias strip. The same instructions can be used to cut bias for piping.

To estimate size of square needed, use this formula:

Length of bias strip needed	×	Width of bias strip	=	Area of strip
Square root of area of strip	=	Size of square to be cut		

1. Cut the determined fabric square. Then cut the square in half diagonally. Sew the resulting triangles together as shown, using a ¼″ seam allowance. Press the seam open.

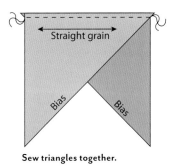

Straight grain

Bias   Bias

Sew triangles together.

2. Using a ruler, mark the parallelogram created by the 2 triangles with lines spaced the width you need to cut the bias strip. We draw our lines 2¼″ apart. Cut about 5″ along the first line.

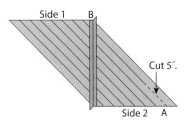

Side 1   B

Cut 5″.

Side 2   A

Mark lines and begin cut.

3. Join Side 1 and Side 2 to form a tube. The raw edge at line A will align with the raw edge at B. This will allow the first line to be offset by a strip width. Pin the raw edges right sides together, making sure that the lines match. Sew with a ¼″ seam allowance. Press the seam open. Cut along the drawn lines, creating a single continuous strip.

4. Fold the entire strip in half lengthwise with wrong sides together. Place binding on quilt as described in Double-Fold Straight-Grain Binding (page 11).

See Finishing the Binding Ends (below) for tips on finishing and hiding the raw edges of the ends of the binding.

FINISHING THE BINDING ENDS

Method 1

After stitching around the quilt, fold under the beginning tail of the binding strip ¼″ so that the raw edge will be inside the binding after it is turned to the back side of the quilt. Place the end tail of the binding strip inside the beginning folded end. Continue to attach the binding and stitch slightly beyond the starting stitches. Trim the excess binding. Fold the binding over the raw edges to the quilt back and hand stitch, mitering the corners.

Method 2

See the tip at www.ctpub.com > Resources > Consumer Resources: Quiltmaking Basics > Quilting Tips: Completing a Binding with an Invisible Seam.

1. Fold the ending tail of the binding back on itself where it meets the beginning binding tail. From the fold, measure and mark the cut width of the binding strip. Cut the ending binding tail to this measurement. For example, if the binding is cut 2¼″ wide, measure 2¼″ from the fold on the ending tail of the binding and cut the binding tail to this length.

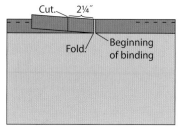

Cut binding tail.

2. Open both tails. Place a tail on top of the other tail at right angles, right sides together. Mark a diagonal line from corner to corner and stitch on the line. Check that you've done it correctly and that the binding fits the quilt; then trim the seam allowance to ¼″. Press open.

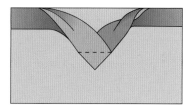

Stitch ends of binding diagonally.

3. Refold the binding and stitch this binding section in place on the quilt. Fold the binding over the raw edges to the quilt back and hand stitch.

Designed, pieced, and quilted by Natalia Bonner and Kathleen Whiting
Fabric shown: Dainty Blossoms by Carina Gardner for Riley Blake Designs

Alternating Stars

Alternating Stars is a striking quilt that appears to be two different blocks, a Pinwheel and an Eight-Pointed Star. It's really one large block with an eight-pointed star at the center. The block's corners form pinwheels when the blocks are set together. The secret is in the fabric placement!

This is a great quilt to show off two of your favorite prints or even two different solid colors and a background color.

Materials

Yardage is based on 42″-wide fabric.

Finished size	BABY 45″ × 45″	THROW 60″ × 60″	COVERLET 75″ × 90″
BLUE FABRIC	1¼ yards	1⅞ yards	3¼ yards
BROWN FABRIC	1 yard	1¾ yards	2½ yards
WHITE FABRIC	1⅛ yards	1¾ yards	3 yards
BACKING FABRIC	3 yards	4 yards	5½ yards
BINDING FABRIC	⅓ yard	½ yard	¾ yard
BATTING	53″ × 53″	68″ × 68″	83″ × 98″

Cutting

Cut the squares diagonally once or twice as indicated by the symbols.

Cut		BABY 9 BLOCKS	THROW 16 BLOCKS	COVERLET 30 BLOCKS
from BLUE FABRIC	3⅜″ × 3⅜″ squares	18	32	60
	3⅜″ × 3⅜″ squares	90 (180 triangles)	160 (320 triangles)	300 (600 triangles)
from BROWN FABRIC	6¼″ × 6¼″ squares	9 (36 triangles)	16 (64 triangles)	30 (120 triangles)
	3⅜″ × 3⅜″ squares	36	64	120
	3⅜″ × 3⅜″ squares	18 (36 triangles)	32 (64 triangles)	60 (120 triangles)
from WHITE FABRIC	6¼″ × 6¼″ squares	9 (36 triangles)	16 (64 triangles)	30 (120 triangles)
	3⅜″ × 3⅜″ squares	18	32	60
	4″ × 4″ squares	36	64	120

Sewing the Block

To make an Alternating Stars block, follow these steps. Seam allowances are ¼″ unless otherwise indicated. Follow the pressing arrows.

Alternating Stars block

1. Use a brown 3⅜″ × 3⅜″ square and a blue 3⅜″ × 3⅜″ square to create 2 half-square triangles, using the No-Waste Method (page 7). Make a total of 4 half-square triangles (Figure A).

2. Sew the 4 half-square triangles together in pairs, and then sew the pairs together to create a pinwheel as shown (Figure B).

A.   **B.**

3. Sew a brown 3⅜″ triangle and 3 blue 3⅜″ triangles to the sides of a 4″ × 4″ white square as shown. Make 4 (Figure C).

> **tip** For best results, sew opposite sides first and press before sewing the remaining two sides.

C.   **D.**

4. Sew a brown 3⅜″ × 3⅜″ square and a white 3⅜″ × 3⅜″ square together to make 2 half-square triangles. Make a total of 4 half-square triangles (Figure D).

5. Sew a blue 3⅜″ triangle to each brown side of the half-square triangle from Step 4 as shown. Make 4 (Figure E).

E.

6. Sew a brown 6¼″ triangle and a white 6¼″ triangle together, matching the short sides as shown. Make 4 (Figure F).

F.

7. Sew the triangle unit from Step 6 to the unit from Step 5. Make 4 (Figure G).

8. Sew 2 units from Step 7 to the unit from Step 3. Note the position of the brown triangle in the center unit. Make 2 (Figure H).

G.

9. Sew a unit from Step 3 onto each side of the pinwheel from Step 2, again noting the position of the brown triangle (Figure I).

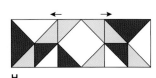

H.

10. Refer to the Alternating Stars block diagram (above) and sew the 3 block sections together.

11. Repeat these steps to make the number of blocks needed (*baby size:* 9 blocks; *throw:* 16 blocks; *coverlet:* 30 blocks).

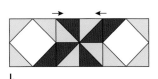

I.

Putting It All Together

Refer to the *Alternating Stars* quilt assembly diagram to find the size quilt you are making. For the baby size, sew 3 rows of 3 blocks. For the throw, sew 4 rows of 4 blocks. For the coverlet, sew 6 rows of 5 blocks. Always press the seams in alternating directions from row to row.

Finishing

Refer to Finishing the Quilt (page 11) for instructions on layering, quilting, and binding the quilt.

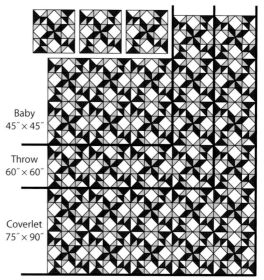

Baby
45″ × 45″

Throw
60″ × 60″

Coverlet
75″ × 90″

Alternating Stars **quilt assembly diagram**

Alternating Stars **coverlet, 75″ × 90″**

Designed, pieced, and quilted by Natalia Bonner and Kathleen Whiting
Fabric shown: Mod Basics by Birch Fabrics

A-Maze Me

FINISHED SIZE: 99″ × 99″ **I BLOCK SIZE:** 16½″ × 16½″

A-Maze Me is a fun geometric block that creates a secondary pattern when the blocks are set together. We've made our version in only three colors, but it would be darling with each block in a different color scheme.

Materials

Yardage is based on 42″-wide fabric.

Finished size	BABY 33″ × 33″	THROW 66″ × 66″	COVERLET 99″ × 99″
ASSORTED YELLOW FABRICS	⅜ yard	1¼ yards	2⅝ yards
ASSORTED WHITE FABRICS	⅝ yard	1⅝ yards	3⅝ yards
ASSORTED GRAY FABRICS	¾ yard	2⅝ yards	5⅝ yards
BACKING FABRIC	1¼ yards	4⅛ yards	9 yards
BINDING FABRIC	½ yard	⅝ yard	¾ yard
BATTING	41″ × 41″	74″ × 74″	107″ × 107″

Cutting

Cut			BABY 4 BLOCKS	THROW 16 BLOCKS	COVERLET 36 BLOCKS
from YELLOW FABRIC		2″ × 12½″ strips	12	48	108
		2″ × 8″ strips	4	16	36
from WHITE FABRIC		2″ × 2″ squares	44	176	396
		2″ × 8″ strips 2″ × 6½″ strips 2″ × 5″ strips	8 of each	32 of each	72 of each
		2″ × 17″ strips	8	32	72
from GRAY FABRIC		2″ × 2″ squares	44	176	396
		2″ × 8″ strips 2″ × 14″ strips 2″ × 6½″ strips	4 of each	16 of each	36 of each
		2″ × 5″ strips	8	32	72

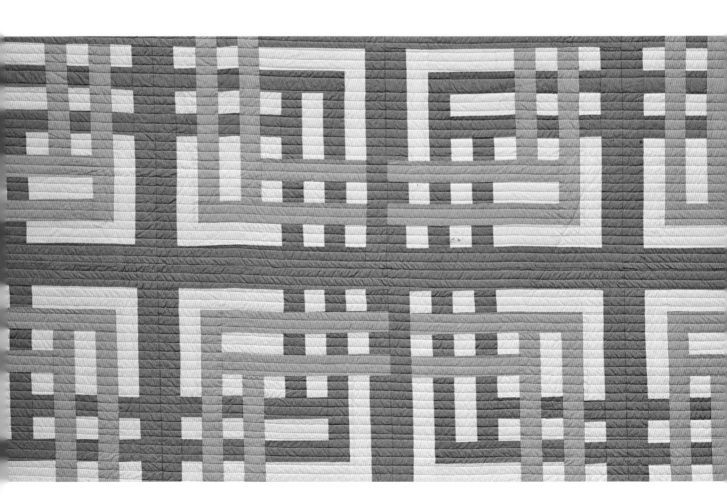

Sewing the Block

To make an A-Maze Me block, follow these steps. Seam allowances are ¼" unless otherwise indicated. Follow the pressing arrows.

> **tip** You could use the method in Strip Piecing (page 8) to make the units in Steps 1, 2, 5, 7, 9, 12, and 14.

1. Sew a white 2" × 2" square to opposite sides of a gray 2" × 2" square (Figure A).

2. Sew 2 gray 2" × 5" strips to opposite sides of a white 2" × 5" strip. Then sew this unit to the unit from Step 1 as shown (Figure B).

3. Sew a gray 2" × 6½" strip to the unit from Step 2 (Figure C).

4. Sew a white 2" × 6½" strip to the unit from Step 3. Set aside (Figure D).

5. Sew a white 2" × 8" strip and a gray 2" × 8" strip together along the long edges.

6. Sew the strip set from Step 5 to the top of the unit from Step 4, and sew a yellow 2" × 8" strip to the bottom of the unit as shown (Figure E).

7. Sew 3 white 2" × 2" squares and 2 gray 2" × 2" squares together (Figure F).

8. Sew the strip set from Step 7 to the yellow side of the unit from Step 6 (Figure G).

9. Sew 2 white and 3 gray 2" × 2" squares together and add a white 2" × 5" strip to an end as shown (Figure H).

10. Sew a yellow 2" × 12½" strip to each long side of the strip set from Step 9 (Figure I).

11. Sew the strip set from Step 10 to the unit from Step 8 (Figure J).

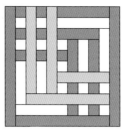

A-Maze Me block

A.   B.

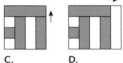

C.   D.

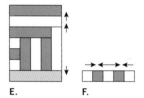

E.   F.

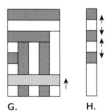

G.   H.

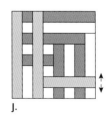

I.   J.

12. Sew 3 gray and 2 white 2″ × 2″ squares together and add a white 2″ × 6½″ strip to an end as shown (Figure K).

13. Sew a yellow 2″ × 12½″ strip to the bottom of the unit from Step 11. Then sew the strip set from Step 12 to the unit as shown (Figure L).

14. Sew 2 white and 2 gray 2″ × 2″ squares together and add a 2″ × 8″ white strip to an end. Then sew a gray 2″ × 14″ strip to the strip set (Figure M).

15. Sew the unit from Step 14 to the unit from Step 13 (Figure N).

16. Refer to the A-Maze Me block diagram (page 21) and sew a 2″ × 17″ gray strip onto opposite sides of the unit from Step 15 to complete the block.

17. Repeat these steps to make the number of blocks needed (*baby size:* 4 blocks; *throw:* 16 blocks; *coverlet:* 36 blocks).

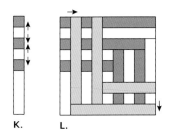

K. L.

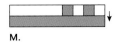

M.

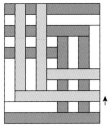

N.

Putting It All Together

Refer to the *A-Maze Me* quilt assembly diagram to find the quilt size you are making. Note the block rotation in the rows. For the baby size, sew 2 rows of 2 blocks. For the throw, sew 4 rows of 4 blocks. For the coverlet, sew 6 rows of 6 blocks. Always press the seams in alternating directions from row to row.

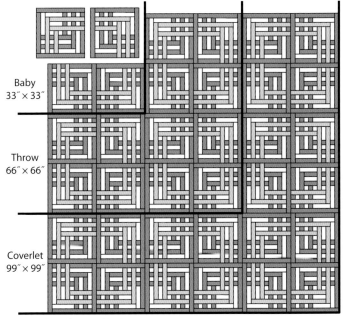

Baby
33″ × 33″

Throw
66″ × 66″

Coverlet
99″ × 99″

A-Maze Me **quilt assembly diagram**

Finishing

Refer to Finishing the Quilt (page 11) for instructions on layering, quilting, and binding the quilt.

A-Maze Me coverlet, 99″ × 99″

Designed and quilted by Natalia Bonner and Kathleen Whiting;
pieced by Ilene Peterson

Fabric shown: Basics by Riley Blake Designs

American Stars

FINISHED SIZE: 68″ × 85″ | **BLOCK SIZE:** 12″ × 12″

American Stars is a twist on a traditional star quilt block. In gray and white, it has a very modern vibe. This quilt would also be a knock-out sewn in prints to achieve a more traditional look.

At first glance, it may look as though this quilt was assembled with sashing. We framed the central star with extra-large corners and Flying Geese units to achieve this effect in just one block. Because it's set on point, there are half-blocks.

Materials

Yardage is based on 42″-wide fabric.

Finished size	BABY 34″ × 34″	THROW 51″ × 68″	COVERLET 68″ × 85″
GRAY FABRIC	1¼ yards	2½ yards	3¾ yards
WHITE FABRIC	1⅝ yards	3¾ yards	5¾ yards
BACKING FABRIC	1¼ yards	3⅓ yards	5¼ yards
BINDING FABRIC	⅜ yard	⅝ yard	¾ yard
BATTING	42″ × 42″	59″ × 76″	76″ × 93″

Cutting

Cut the squares twice diagonally as indicated by the symbols.

Cut		BABY 4 BLOCKS, 8 HALF-BLOCKS	THROW 17 BLOCKS, 14 HALF-BLOCKS	COVERLET 31 BLOCKS, 18 HALF-BLOCKS
from GRAY FABRIC	⊠ 7″ × 7″ squares	2 (8 triangles)	4 (14 triangles)	5 (18 triangles)
	2½″ × 4½″ squares	32	96	160
	4½″ × 4½″ squares	4	17	31
	2½″ × 2½″ squares	64	192	320
from WHITE FABRIC	⊠ 7″ × 7″ squares	4 (16 triangles)	7 (28 triangles)	9 (36 triangles)
	2½″ × 4½″ rectangles	32	96	160
	4½″ × 4½″ squares	24	82	142
	2½″ × 2½″ squares	64	192	320

Sewing the Block

To make an American Stars block and an American Stars half-block, follow these steps. Seam allowances are ¼" unless otherwise indicated. Refer to Flying Geese (page 8) to see additional block assembly options. Follow the pressing arrows.

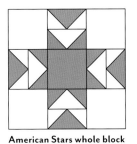

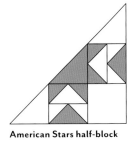

American Stars whole block   **American Stars half-block**

1. Refer to the Easy Sew Method for Flying Geese (page 9). Use 2 white 2½" × 2½" squares and a gray 2½" × 4½" rectangle to make a Flying Geese unit. Make 4 for the whole block and make 2 for the half-block (Figure A).

A.

2. Use 2 gray 2½" × 2½" squares and a white 2½" × 4½" rectangle to make a Flying Geese unit. Make 4 for the whole block and make 2 for the half-block (Figure B).

B.

3. Sew the Flying Geese units from Steps 1 and 2 together (Figure C).

C.

4. Sew 2 white 4½″ × 4½″ squares to opposite sides of a unit from Step 3. Make 2 for the whole block (Figure D).

5. Sew 2 units from Step 3 to opposite sides of a gray 4½″ × 4½″ square (Figure E).

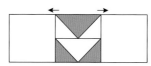

D.

6. Referring to the American Stars whole block diagram (previous page), sew a unit from Step 4 to the top and the bottom of the unit from Step 5 to complete a whole block.

7. For the half-block, sew a white 4½″ × 4½″ square, a Flying Geese unit from Step 3, and a white triangle together as shown (Figure F).

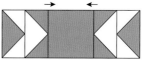

E.

8. Sew a Flying Geese unit from Step 3 and a gray triangle together (Figure G).

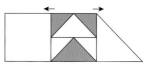

F.

9. Referring to the American Stars half-block diagram (previous page), sew the unit from Step 7 and the unit from Step 8 together. Then add a white triangle to the side of the Flying Geese unit to complete a half-block.

G.

10. Repeat these steps to make the number of blocks needed (*baby size:* 4 whole blocks and 8 half-blocks; *throw:* 17 whole blocks and 14 half-blocks; *coverlet:* 31 whole blocks and 18 half-blocks).

Putting It All Together

Refer to the *American Stars* quilt assembly diagrams to find the size quilt you are making. Arrange the whole blocks and half-blocks in diagonal rows. Sew each row together. Always press the seams in alternating directions from row to row.

American Stars **baby quilt assembly diagram, finished 34″ × 34″**

American Stars **throw quilt assembly diagram, finished 51″ × 68″**

American Stars **coverlet quilt assembly diagram, finished 68″ × 85″**

Finishing

Refer to Finishing the Quilt (page 11) for instructions
on layering, quilting, and binding the quilt.

American Stars coverlet, 68″ × 85″

Designed and quilted by Natalia Bonner and Kathleen Whiting;
pieced by Ainslee Howells

Fabric shown: Heaven and Helsinki by Patty Young for
Michael Miller Fabrics

Bouncing

FINISHED SIZE: *75″ × 88″* | **BLOCK SIZE:** *12½″ × 12½″*

Materials

Yardage is based on 42"-wide fabric.

Finished size	BABY 50″ × 50″	THROW 63″ × 63″	COVERLET 75″ × 88″
PURPLE FABRIC	¼ yard	⅝ yard	¾ yard
ORANGE FABRIC	¼ yard	⅝ yard	¾ yard
GREEN FABRIC	¼ yard	⅝ yard	¾ yard
BROWN FABRIC	¼ yard	⅝ yard	¾ yard
PINK FABRIC	¼ yard	⅝ yard	¾ yard
WHITE FABRIC	2¼ yards	3½ yards	5⅜ yards
BACKING FABRIC	3¼ yards	4 yards	5⅓ yards
BINDING FABRIC	½ yard	½ yard	¾ yard
BATTING	58″ × 58″	71″ × 71″	83″ × 96″

This is such a happy quilt; wouldn't it look cheery on a nursery wall? We love the illusion of movement that is created by the shift of the print rectangles in each block. The almost-square white rectangles are unexpected, giving a modern flair and additional movement to this design.

Cutting

Cut		BABY 16 BLOCKS	THROW 25 BLOCKS	COVERLET 42 BLOCKS
from PURPLE FABRIC	1¼″ × 6″ strips	14	20	34
	1¼″ × 6¾″ strips	14	20	34
from ORANGE FABRIC	1¼″ × 6″ strips	16	20	34
	1¼″ × 6¾″ strips	16	20	34
from GREEN FABRIC	1¼″ × 6″ strips	12	20	34
	1¼″ × 6¾″ strips	12	20	34
from BROWN FABRIC	1¼″ × 6″ strips	10	20	32
	1¼″ × 6¾″ strips	10	20	32
from PINK FABRIC	1¼″ × 6″ strips	12	20	34
	1¼″ × 6¾″ strips	12	20	34
from WHITE FABRIC	1¼″ × 1¼″ squares	128	200	336
	6″ × 6¾″ rectangles	32	50	84
	5¼″ × 6″ rectangles	32	50	84

tip You could use the method in Strip Piecing (page 8) to make the units in Step 2.

Sewing the Block

To make a Bouncing block, follow these steps. Seam allowances are ¼″ unless otherwise indicated. Follow the pressing arrows.

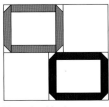

Bouncing block

1. Using the white 1¼″ × 1¼″ squares, make snowball corners (page 7) on each end of 2 matching-color 1¼″ × 6¾″ strips. Repeat with a contrasting set of 2 matching-color 1¼″ × 6¾″ strips (Figure A).

A.

2. Sew matching-color 1¼″ × 6″ strips to both long sides of a white 5¼″ × 6″ piece. Repeat with matching-color strips and another white 5¼″ × 6″ piece (Figure B).

B.

3. Sew matching-color strips from Step 1 to the units from Step 2 (Figure C).

4. Sew a white 6″ × 6¾″ rectangle to the side of each unit from Step 3 as shown (Figure D).

C.

5. Referring to the Bouncing block diagram, sew the units from Step 4 together, with the color units at opposite ends of the rows, to complete the block.

6. Repeat these steps to make the number of blocks needed (*baby size:* 16 blocks; *throw:* 25 blocks; *coverlet:* 42 blocks).

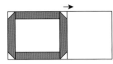

D.

Putting It All Together

> **tip** For best results, put the colors together randomly. This pattern is designed to look scrappy, so have fun with it.

Refer to the *Bouncing* quilt assembly diagram to find the size quilt you are making. For the baby size, sew 4 rows of 4 blocks. For the throw, sew 5 rows of 5 blocks. For the coverlet, sew 7 rows of 6 blocks. Always press the seams in alternating directions from row to row.

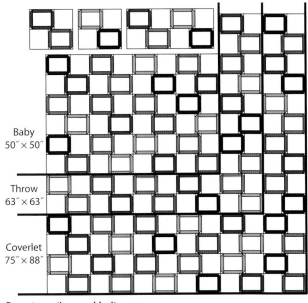

Baby
50″ × 50″

Throw
63″ × 63″

Coverlet
75″ × 88″

Bouncing **quilt assembly diagram**

Finishing

Refer to Finishing the Quilt (page 11) for instructions
on layering, quilting, and binding the quilt.

Bouncing coverlet, 75″ × 88″

Designed, pieced, and quilted by Natalia Bonner and Kathleen Whiting
Fabrics shown: Madrona Road by Violet Craft for Michael Miller Fabrics

Bow Ties

FINISHED SIZE: 89″ × 89″ | **BLOCK SIZE:** 9″ × 9″

Materials

Yardage is based on 42″-wide fabric.

Bow Ties is a fun, template-pieced quilt. Some of the pieces are small, but the end result is worth the time. When these blocks are set together in diagonal rows, they create a secondary diagonal pattern that elevates this quilt to a new interest level.

Finished size	BABY 51″ × 51″	THROW 64″ × 64″	COVERLET 89″ × 89″
PINK FABRIC	1⅜ yards	2⅛ yards	4¼ yards
WHITE FABRIC	3 yards	4 yards	7¼ yards
BACKING FABRIC	3⅓ yards	4 yards	8⅛ yards
BINDING FABRIC	½ yard	½ yard	¾ yard
BATTING	59″ × 59″	72″ × 72″	97″ × 97″

Cutting

Copy the Bow Ties *patterns A/Ar and B (page 37) at 100%. Refer to Template Piecing (page 10) for instructions on cutting the indicated pieces. Cut the squares diagonally twice as indicated by the symbol.*

Cut		BABY 25 BLOCKS	THROW 41 BLOCKS	COVERLET 85 BLOCKS
from PINK FABRIC	3½″ × 3½″ squares	25	41	85
	Template B	100	164	340
from WHITE FABRIC	14″ × 14″ squares	3 (12 triangles)	4 (16 triangles)	6 (24 triangles)
	Template A	100	164	340
	Template Ar	100	164	340
	3½″ × 3½″ squares	100	164	340
	1⅝″ × 1⅝″ squares	100	164	340

Sewing the Block

To make a Bow Ties block, follow these steps. Refer to Template Piecing (page 10) for tips on using this method. Seam allowances are ¼" unless otherwise indicated. Follow the pressing arrows.

1. Make 4 A/B/Ar units as shown (Figure A).

2. Using the white 1⅝" × 1⅝" squares, sew snowball corners (page 7) onto all 4 corners of a pink 3½" × 3½" square (Figure B).

3. Sew 2 units from Step 1 to opposite sides of the unit from Step 2 as shown. Set aside (Figure C).

4. Sew 2 white 3½" × 3½" squares to opposite sides of a unit from Step 1 as shown. Make 2 (Figure D).

5. Referring to the Bow Ties block diagram, sew a unit from Step 4 to the top and the bottom of the unit from Step 3 to complete the block.

6. Repeat these steps to make the number of blocks needed (*baby size:* 25 blocks; *throw:* 41 blocks; *coverlet:* 85 blocks).

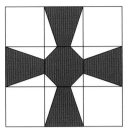

Bow Ties block

A.   **B.**

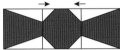

C.

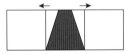

D.

Putting It All Together

Refer to the *Bow Ties* quilt assembly diagrams to find the size quilt you are making. Arrange the blocks and white setting triangles in diagonal rows. Sew each row together. For the baby size, use 25 blocks and 12 white setting triangles. For the throw, use 41 blocks and 16 white setting triangles. For the coverlet, use 85 blocks and 24 white setting triangles. Always press the seams in alternating directions from row to row.

Bow Ties **baby quilt assembly diagram, finished 51" × 51"**

Bow Ties **throw quilt assembly diagram, finished 64" × 64"**

Bow Ties **coverlet quilt assembly diagram, finished 89" × 89"**

Finishing

Refer to Finishing the Quilt (page 11) for instructions on layering, quilting, and binding the quilt.

Bow Ties
A and Ar

Bow Ties
B

Bow Ties coverlet, 89″ × 89″

Designed and quilted by Natalia Bonner and Kathleen Whiting;
pieced by Emmy Jasperson

Fabrics shown: Mod Basics by Birch Fabrics and Avalon by
Jay-Cyn Designs for Birch Fabrics

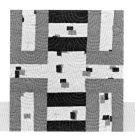

Buckle Up

FINISHED SIZE: 95″ × 95″ **|** **BLOCK SIZE:** 15¾″ × 15¾″

This quilt is so easy to make! Made in one of the smaller sizes, it would be a great gift for someone who needs a lap quilt. And what fun for an easy baby quilt that could be thrown on the floor for baby to play on.

In our three-color version, *Buckle Up* has a simple but bold look. To give it a softer dimension, try making it in multiple colors.

Materials

Yardage is based on 42″-wide fabric.

Finished size	BABY 47″ × 47″	THROW 63″ × 63″	COVERLET 95″ × 95″
BLUE FABRIC	¾ yard	⅞ yard	1⅝ yards
GREEN FABRIC	1¼ yards	2⅛ yards	4½ yards
WHITE PRINT FABRIC	1½ yards	2 yards	4¼ yards
BACKING FABRIC	3⅛ yards	4 yards	8⅝ yards
BINDING FABRIC	⅜ yard	½ yard	¾ yard
BATTING	55″ × 55″	71″ × 71″	103″ × 103″

Cutting

tip You could use the method in Strip Piecing (page 8) to make the units in Steps 1 and 3.

Cut		BABY 9 BLOCKS	THROW 16 BLOCKS	COVERLET 36 BLOCKS
from BLUE FABRIC	2¼″ × 5¾″ strips	36	64	144
from GREEN FABRIC	2¼″ × 5¾″ strips	108	192	432
from WHITE FABRIC	2¼″ × 5¾″ strips	72	128	288
	2¼″ × 16¼″ strips	9	16	36

Sewing the Block

To make a Buckle Up block, follow these steps. Seam allowances are ¼" unless otherwise indicated. Follow the pressing arrows.

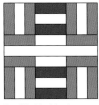

Buckle Up block

1. Sew a green 2¼" × 5¾" strip onto the 2 long sides of a white 2¼" × 5¾" strip. Make 4 (Figure A).

A.

2. Sew a green 2¼" × 5¾" strip onto an end of the strip set from Step 1. Make 4 (Figure B).

B.

3. Sew 2 blue 2¼" × 5¾" strips and 2 white 2¼" × 5¾" strips together as shown. Make 2 (Figure C).

C.

4. Sew 2 units from Step 2 to opposite sides of a strip set from Step 3. Make 2 (Figure D).

5. Referring to the Buckle Up block diagram, sew a unit from Step 4 to each long side of a white 2¼" × 16¼" strip to complete the block.

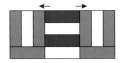

D.

6. Repeat these steps to make the number of blocks needed (*baby size:* 9 blocks; *throw:* 16 blocks; *coverlet:* 36 blocks).

Putting It All Together

Refer to the *Buckle Up* quilt assembly diagram to find the size quilt you are making. For the baby size, sew 3 rows of 3 blocks. For the throw, sew 4 rows of 4 blocks. For the coverlet, sew 6 rows of 6 blocks. Always press the seams in alternating directions from row to row.

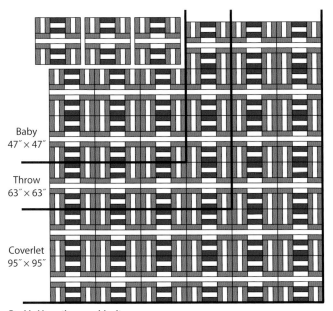

Baby
47″ × 47″

Throw
63″ × 63″

Coverlet
95″ × 95″

***Buckle Up* quilt assembly diagram**

Finishing

Refer to Finishing the Quilt (page 11) for instructions
on layering, quilting, and binding the quilt.

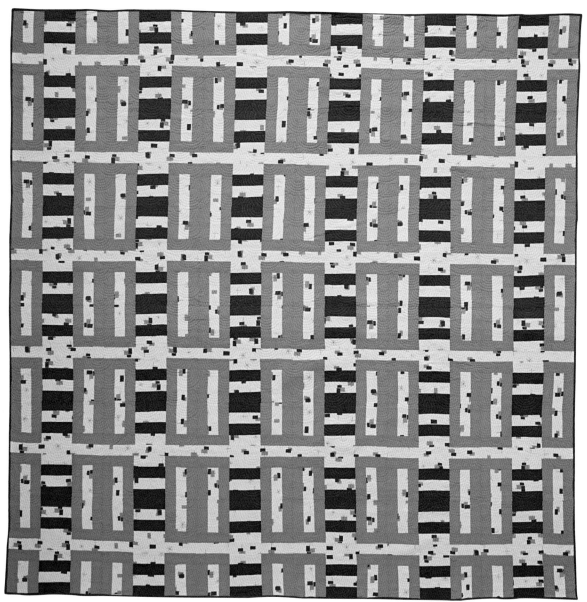

Buckle Up coverlet, 95″ × 95″

Designed and quilted by Natalia Bonner and Kathleen Whiting;
pieced by Ilene Peterson

Fabric shown: Kona Cottons by Robert Kaufman Fabrics

Cabana

FINISHED SIZE: *72″ × 84″* **| BLOCK SIZE:** *12″ × 12″*

We love this quilt because the simple template pattern contains a bit of a puzzle—the tops of the cabanas are pieced into the blocks in the row above each row of cabana bodies. The result is a quilt that looks complicated. But large templates make piecing this unusual quilt really quick and easy.

This version is made in ivory with four shades of brown. For the same simple piecing but a bigger challenge in color planning, you could make each cabana a different print.

Materials

Yardage is based on 42″-wide fabric.

Finished size	BABY 48″ × 48″	THROW 60″ × 60″	COVERLET 72″ × 84″
▪ DARK BROWN FABRIC	½ yard	1⅛ yards	1⅜ yards
▪ BROWN FABRIC	½ yard	¾ yard	1⅜ yard
▪ MEDIUM BROWN FABRIC	½ yard	¾ yard	1⅜ yards
▪ LIGHT BROWN FABRIC	½ yard	¾ yard	1⅜ yards
□ IVORY FABRIC	1⅝ yards	2¼ yards	3⅝ yards
BACKING FABRIC	3⅛ yards	3⅞ yards	5⅛ yards
BINDING FABRIC	½ yard	½ yard	¾ yard
BATTING	56″ × 56″	68″ × 68″	80″ × 92″

Cutting

Copy the Cabana *patterns A–D (pages 46 and 47) at 100%. Join the B/B and C/C split templates along the dashed join lines. Refer to Template Piecing (page 10) for instructions on cutting the indicated pieces.*

Cut		BABY 16 BLOCKS	THROW 25 BLOCKS	COVERLET 42 BLOCKS
▪ *from* DARK BROWN FABRIC	Templates A and Ar	4 of each	5 of each	6 of each
	Templates C and Cr	4 of each	10 of each	12 of each
▪ *from* BROWN FABRIC	Templates A and Ar	4 of each	10 of each	12 of each
	Templates C and Cr	4 of each	5 of each	12 of each
▪ *from* MEDIUM BROWN FABRIC	Templates A and Ar	4 of each	5 of each	12 of each
	Templates C and Cr	4 of each	5 of each	12 of each
▪ *from* LIGHT BROWN FABRIC	Templates A and Ar	4 of each	5 of each	12 of each
	Templates C and Cr	4 of each	5 of each	6 of each
□ *from* IVORY FABRIC	Templates B and Br	16 of each	25 of each	42 of each
	Templates D and Dr	16 of each	25 of each	42 of each

Sewing the Block

> **tip** Take some time to plan color placement before sewing this quilt. The tops of the cabanas are created when you sew the blocks and rows together—the template A and Ar pieces at the bottom outside corners of each block form the tops of the cabanas in the row below.
>
> Use a design wall or large floor area to lay fabric out for color placement.
>
> If you want to make each cabana from a different fabric, take note that each block contains two half-cabanas. You will need to match fabrics to the row above and to the blocks on either side.

Cabana block

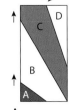

A.

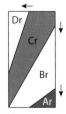

B.

To make a Cabana block, follow these steps. Refer to Template Piecing (page 10) for tips on using this method. Seam allowances are ¼" unless otherwise indicated. Follow the pressing arrows.

1. Make an A/B/C/D unit as shown (Figure A).

2. Make an Ar/Br/Cr/Dr unit as shown (Figure B).

3. Referring to the Cabana block diagram, sew units from Steps 1 and 2 together to complete the block.

4. Repeat these steps to make the number of blocks needed (*baby size:* 16 blocks; *throw:* 25 blocks; *coverlet:* 42 blocks).

Putting It All Together

Refer to the *Cabana* quilt assembly diagram to find the size quilt that you are making. Note the block color placement within the rows. For the baby size, sew 4 rows of 4 blocks. For the throw, sew 5 rows of 5 blocks. For the coverlet, sew 7 rows of 6 blocks. Always press the seams in alternating directions from row to row.

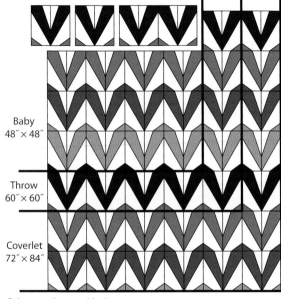

Baby
48″ × 48″

Throw
60″ × 60″

Coverlet
72″ × 84″

***Cabana* quilt assembly diagram**

Finishing

Refer to Finishing the Quilt (page 11) for instructions
on layering, quilting, and binding the quilt.

Cabana coverlet, 72″ × 84″

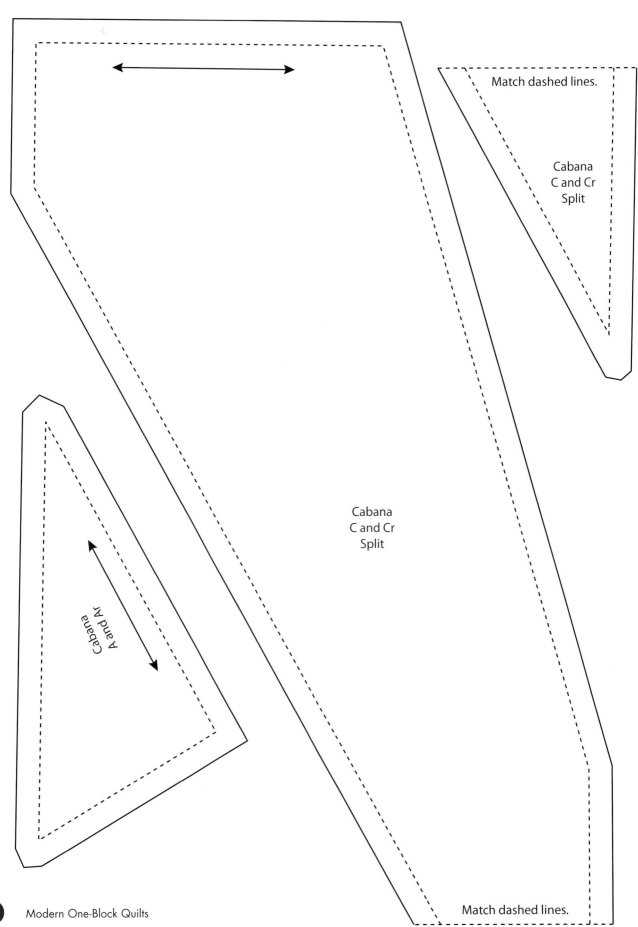

Match dashed lines.

Cabana
C and Cr
Split

Cabana
C and Cr
Split

Cabana
A and Ar

Match dashed lines.

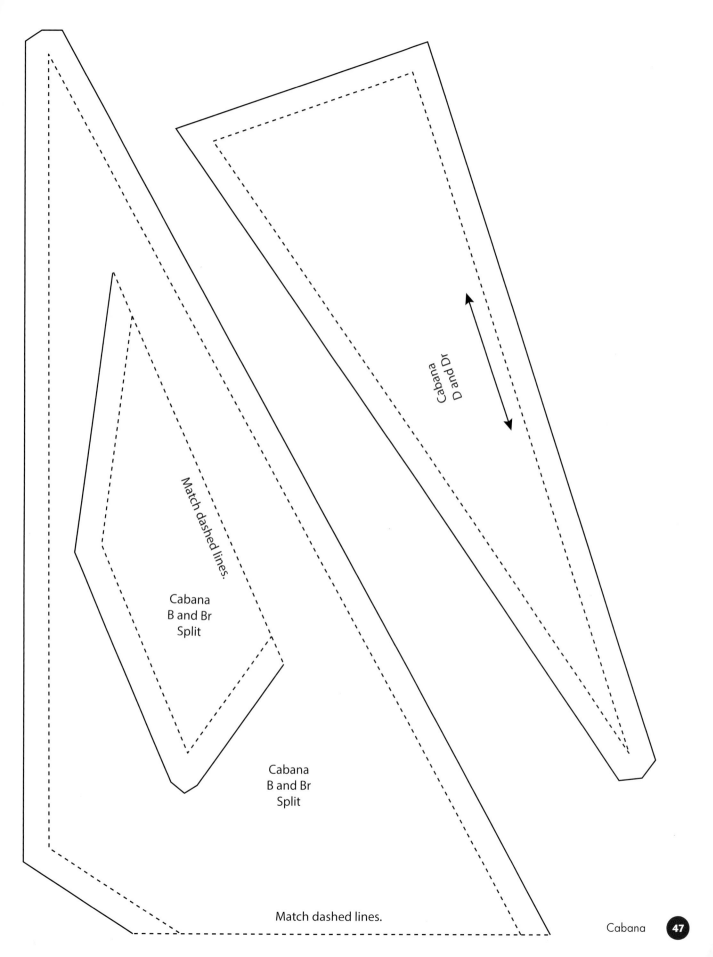

Cabana
D and Dr

Match dashed lines.

Cabana
B and Br
Split

Cabana
B and Br
Split

Match dashed lines.

Designed, pieced, and quilted by Natalia Bonner and Kathleen Whiting
Fabric shown: Lucy's Crab Shack by Sweetwater for Moda Fabrics

Churned

FINISHED SIZE: 80″ × 80″ | **BLOCK SIZE:** 10″ × 10″

Looks are deceiving—in a charming way—in this twist on a traditional *Churn Dash* quilt. We've sewn white strips to just two sides of our Churn Dash block, making the design off-center. The result is a square block that is set in straight, traditional rows even though the quilt looks as if it were put together in a complex diagonal setting.

This pattern would be perfect for a charm quilt or even to use for a block exchange. The fabric colors could be different for each block; the background fabric would need to stay the same to create the illusion of the random setting.

Materials

Yardage is based on 42″-wide fabric.

Finished size	BABY 40″ × 40″	THROW 60″ × 60″	COVERLET 80″ × 80″
DARK BLUE FABRIC	⅜ yard	⅝ yard	1½ yards
LIGHT BLUE FABRIC	⅜ yard	⅝ yard	1½ yards
RED FABRIC	⅜ yard	⅝ yard	1½ yards
ORANGE FABRIC	⅜ yard	⅝ yard	1½ yards
WHITE FABRIC	2 yards	3½ yards	6⅛ yards
BACKING FABRIC	2¾ yards	3⅞ yards	7⅜ yards
BINDING FABRIC	⅜ yard	½ yard	¾ yard
BATTING	48″ × 48″	68″ × 68″	88″ × 88″

Cutting

Cut		BABY 16 BLOCKS	THROW 36 BLOCKS	COVERLET 64 BLOCKS
from DARK BLUE, LIGHT BLUE, RED, and ORANGE FABRICS	3⅜″ × 3⅜″ squares	8 of each color (32)	18 of each color (72)	32 of each color (128)
	1¾″ × 3″ strips	16 of each color (64)	36 of each color (144)	64 of each color (256)
	3″ × 3″ squares	16	36	64
	3⅜″ × 3⅜″ squares	32	72	128
from WHITE FABRIC	1¾″ × 3″ strips	64	144	256
	3″ × 10½″ strips	16	36	64
	3″ × 8″ strips	16	36	64

Sewing the Block

To make a Churned block, follow these steps. Seam allowances are ¼" unless otherwise indicated. Follow the pressing arrows.

1. Use a white 3⅜" × 3⅜" square and a color 3⅜" × 3⅜" square to make 2 half-square triangles, using the No-Waste Method (page 7). Repeat to make a total of 4 matching half-square triangles (Figure A).

2. Use strips that match the color used in Step 1. Sew a color 1¾" × 3" strip to a white 1¾" × 3" strip. Make 4 (Figure B).

> **tip** You could use the method in Strip Piecing (page 8) to make the units in Step 2.

3. Sew 2 units from Step 2 to opposite sides of a white 3" × 3" square (Figure C).

4. Sew matching half-square triangles to each end of a unit from Step 2 as shown. Make 2 (Figure D).

5. Sew the unit from Step 3 between the units from Step 4 as shown (Figure E).

6. Sew a white 3" × 8" strip to the left side of the unit from Step 5 (Figure F).

7. Referring to the Churned block diagram, sew a white 3" × 10½" strip to the bottom of the unit from Step 5 to complete the block.

8. Repeat these steps to make the number of blocks needed (*baby size:* 16 blocks; *throw:* 36 blocks; *coverlet:* 64 blocks).

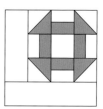

Churned block

A.

B.

C.

D.

E.

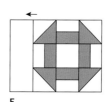

F.

Putting It All Together

Refer to the *Churned* quilt assembly diagram to find the size quilt that you are making. Note the block orientation or rotate the blocks randomly to give a wonky, churned look to the quilt. For the baby size, sew 4 rows of 4 blocks. For the throw, sew 6 rows of 6 blocks. For the coverlet, sew 8 rows of 8 blocks. Always press the seams in alternating directions from row to row.

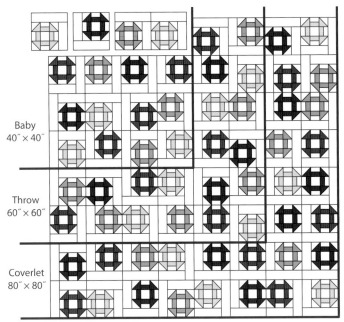

Baby
40˝ × 40˝

Throw
60˝ × 60˝

Coverlet
80˝ × 80˝

Churned **quilt assembly diagram**

Finishing

Refer to Finishing the Quilt (page 11) for instructions on layering, quilting, and binding the quilt.

Churned coverlet, 80″ × 80″

Designed, pieced, and quilted by Natalia Bonner and
Kathleen Whiting

Fabrics shown: Bella Solids by Moda Fabrics and Kona Cottons
by Robert Kaufman Fabrics

Colored Candies

FINISHED SIZE: *72″ × 72″* | **BLOCK SIZE:** *9″ × 9″*

The dark gray background gives this easy quilt the look of modern art. Wouldn't it look delicious hanging on a wall?

Colored Candies is shown in all solids but would be so soft and pretty made with prints surrounding tone-on-tone squares. With large pieces that are simple to sew together, *Colored Candies* would be a very good "first quilt" for a quilting beginner.

Materials

Yardage is based on 42″-wide fabric.

Finished size	BABY 45″ × 45″	THROW 63″ × 63″	COVERLET 72″ × 72″
PINK FABRIC	⅜ yard	½ yard	½ yard
GREEN FABRIC	⅜ yard	½ yard	½ yard
YELLOW FABRIC	⅜ yard	½ yard	½ yard
ORANGE FABRIC	¼ yard	½ yard	½ yard
GRAY FABRIC	2 yards	3¼ yards	4 yards
BACKING FABRIC	3 yards	4 yards	4½ yards
BINDING FABRIC	⅜ yard	½ yard	⅝ yard
BATTING	53″ × 53″	71″ × 71″	80″ × 80″

Cutting

Cut		BABY 12 A and 12 B BLOCKS	THROW 24 A and 25 B BLOCKS	COVERLET 32 A and 32 B BLOCKS
from PINK FABRIC	3½″ × 3½″ squares	13	25	32
from GREEN FABRIC	3½″ × 3½″ squares	13	25	32
from YELLOW FABRIC	3½″ × 3½″ squares	12	24	32
from ORANGE FABRIC	3½″ × 3½″ squares	12	24	32
from GRAY FABRIC	3½″ × 3½″ squares	25	49	64
	3½″ × 9½″ strips	50	98	128

Sewing the Block

To make a Colored Candies block A and a Colored Candies block B, follow these steps. Seam allowances are ¼" unless otherwise indicated. Follow the pressing arrows.

1. Sew a green, a gray, and a pink 3½" × 3½" square together (Figure A).

2. Sew an orange, a gray, and a yellow 3½" × 3½" square together. Set aside (Figure B).

> **tip** You could use the method in Strip Piecing (page 8) to make the units in Steps 1 and 2.

3. Referring to the Colored Candies block diagrams, sew a gray 3½" × 9½" strip to each long side of the strip sets from Steps 1 and 2 to complete blocks A and B.

4. Repeat the steps to make the number of blocks needed (*baby size:* 12 of block A and 13 of block B; *throw:* 24 of block A and 25 of block B; *coverlet:* 32 of block A and 32 of block B).

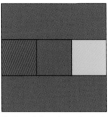

Colored Candies block A

Colored Candies block B

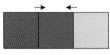

A.

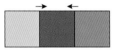

B.

Putting It All Together

Refer to the *Colored Candies* quilt assembly diagram to find the size quilt you are making. Note the orientation of the A and B blocks as they alternate and rotate within each row. For the baby size, sew 5 rows of 5 blocks. For the throw, sew 7 rows of 7 blocks. For the coverlet, sew 8 rows of 8 blocks. Always press the seams in alternating directions from row to row.

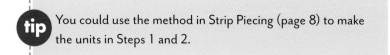

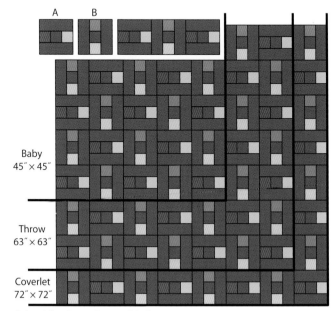

A   B

Baby
45" × 45"

Throw
63" × 63"

Coverlet
72" × 72"

***Colored Candies* quilt assembly diagram**

Finishing

Refer to Finishing the Quilt (page 11) for instructions on layering, quilting, and binding the quilt.

Colored Candies coverlet, 72″ × 72″

Designed and quilted by Natalia Bonner and Kathleen Whiting; pieced by Ashlee Woolf

Fabric shown: Bella Solids by Moda Fabrics

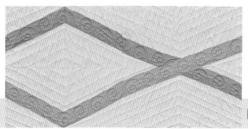

Criss-Cross

FINISHED SIZE: 72″ × 84″ | **BLOCK SIZE:** 24″ × 12″

Zigs and zags dance across the quilt in this lively version of the popular traditional Zigzag pattern. We love the crispness of the white fabric contrasting with the medium green and gray. The combination seems just right for a shabby chic bed with a white painted frame or a more contemporary bed with a white padded headboard.

You could limit the palette even more and make this quilt in just two colors for a look that would be just as vivid. Or do some stash busting and make each zigzagging stripe a different color.

Materials

Yardage is based on 42″-wide fabric.

Finished size		BABY 48″ × 48″	THROW 72″ × 72″	COVERLET 72″ × 84″
	GREEN FABRIC	⅝ yard	1⅛ yards	1⅜ yards
	GRAY FABRIC	⅝ yard	1⅛ yards	1⅜ yards
	IVORY FABRIC	2⅝ yards	5⅛ yards	6¼ yards
BACKING FABRIC		3⅛ yards	4½ yards	5⅛ yards
BINDING FABRIC		⅜ yard	⅝ yard	⅞ yard
BATTING		56″ × 56″	80″ × 80″	80″ × 92″

Cutting

Copy the Criss-Cross *patterns A–J (pages 64–67) and K–L (page 126) at 100%. Join the split patterns at the dashed lines. Refer to Template Piecing (page 10) for instructions on cutting the indicated pieces.*

Cut		BABY 4 A *and* 4 B BLOCKS	THROW 9 A *and* 9 B BLOCKS	COVERLET 11 A *and* 11 B BLOCKS*
from GREEN FABRIC	Templates B and Br	4 of each	9 of each	11 of each
	Templates E and Er	4 of each	9 of each	11 of each
	Template H	4	9	11
	Template K	4	9	11
	Template L	4	9	11
from GRAY FABRIC	Templates B and Br	4 of each	9 of each	11 of each
	Templates E and Er	4 of each	9 of each	11 of each
	Template H	4	9	11
	Template K	4	9	11
	Template L	4	9	11
from WHITE FABRIC	Templates A and Ar	8 of each	18 of each	22 of each
	Templates C and Cr	8 of each	18 of each	22 of each
	Templates D and Dr	8 of each	18 of each	22 of each
	Templates F and Fr	8 of each	18 of each	22 of each
	Templates G and Gr	8 of each	18 of each	22 of each
	Template I	8	18	22
	Template J	8	18	22

* You will have an extra block B.

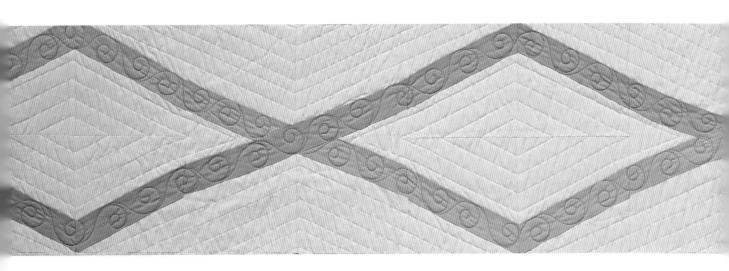

Sewing the Block

After making our quilt, we decided to simplify it for you by eliminating two seams in each block. Use the templates and these illustrations for the simpler construction of the blocks.

To make a Criss-Cross block A and a Criss-Cross block B, follow these steps. Refer to Template Piecing (page 10) for pointers on using this method. Seam allowances are ¼" unless otherwise indicated. Follow the pressing arrows.

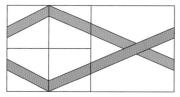

Criss-Cross block A

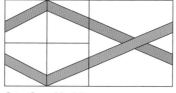

Criss-Cross block B

1. Sew an A/B (gray)/C unit. Sew an A/B (green)/C unit (Figure A).

2. Sew a D/E (gray)/F unit. Sew a D/E (green)/F unit (Figure B).

3. Sew the units from Steps 1 and 2 together as shown (Figure C).

4. Sew an Ar/Br (green)/Cr unit. Sew an Ar/Br (gray)/Cr unit (Figure D).

5. Sew a Dr/Er (green)/Fr unit. Sew a Dr/Er (gray)/Fr unit (Figure E).

6. Sew the units from Steps 4 and 5 together as shown (Figure F).

7. Sew the units from Step 3 to the top of the units from Step 6 as shown. Make 2 (Figure G).

8. Sew a G/H (gray)/I unit. Sew a G/H (green)/I unit (Figure H).

A.

B.

 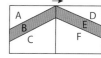

C.

Block A — Block B

D.

E.

 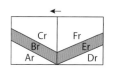

F.

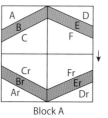 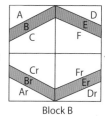

Block A — Block B

G.

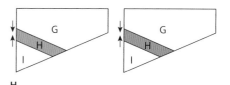

H.

9. Sew a J/K (gray)/Gr unit. Sew a J/K (green)/Gr unit (Figure I).

10. Sew piece L to each J/K/Gr unit (Figure J).

11. Sew the units from Step 8 to the top of the units from Step 10 as shown (Figure K).

12. Referring to the Criss-Cross block diagrams (page 61), sew the units from Step 7 and Step 11 as shown (Figures L and M).

13. Repeat these steps to make the number of blocks needed (*baby size:* 4 block A and 4 block B; *throw:* 9 block A and 9 block B; *coverlet:* 11 block A and 11 block B*).

* You will have an extra block B for a pillow or to piece into the backing.

Putting It All Together

Refer to the *Criss-Cross* quilt assembly diagram to find the size quilt that you are making. Note the placement of the A and B blocks in each row. For the baby size, sew 4 rows of 2 blocks. For the throw, sew 6 rows of 3 blocks. For the coverlet, sew 7 rows of 3 blocks. Always press the seams in alternating directions for row to row.

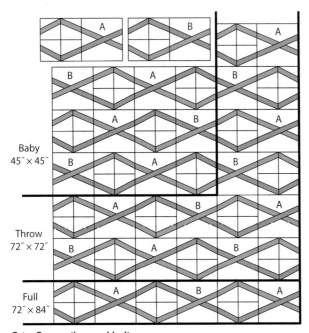

Criss-Cross quilt assembly diagram

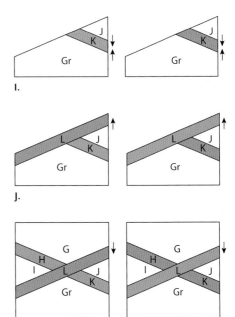

I.

J.

K.

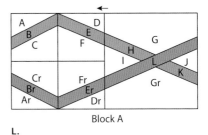

Block A

L.

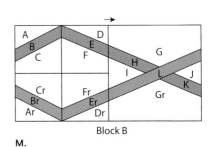

Block B

M.

Finishing

Refer to Finishing the Quilt (page 11) for instructions
on layering, quilting, and binding the quilt.

Criss-Cross coverlet, 72″ × 84″

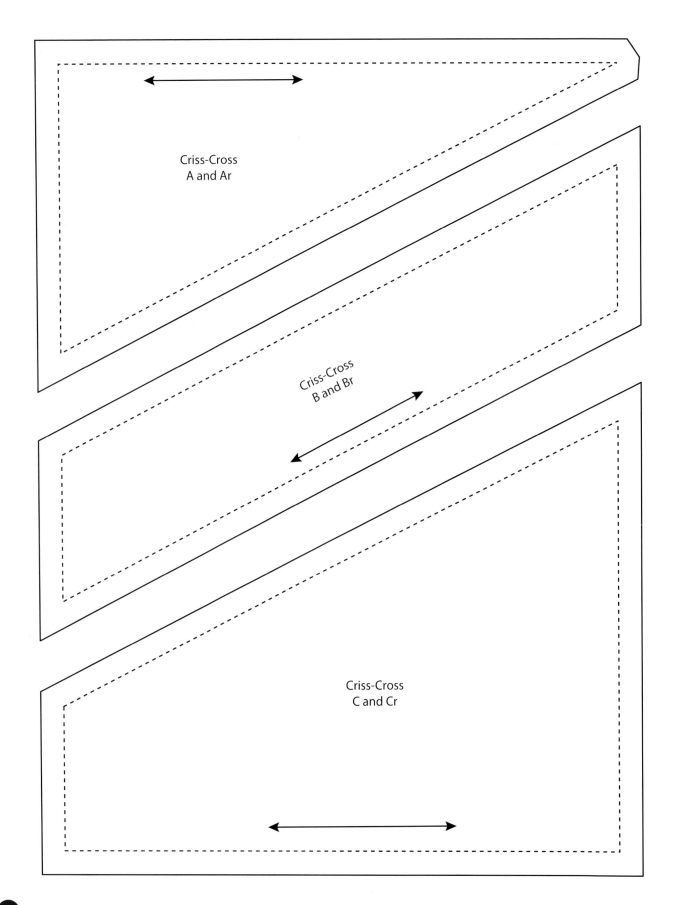

Criss-Cross
A and Ar

Criss-Cross
B and Br

Criss-Cross
C and Cr

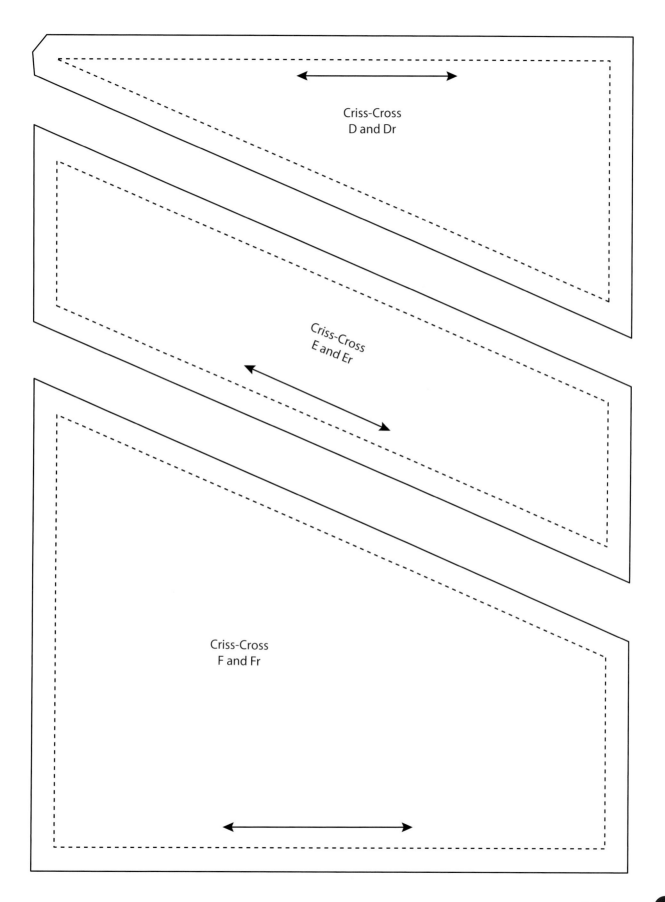

Criss-Cross
D and Dr

Criss-Cross
E and Er

Criss-Cross
F and Fr

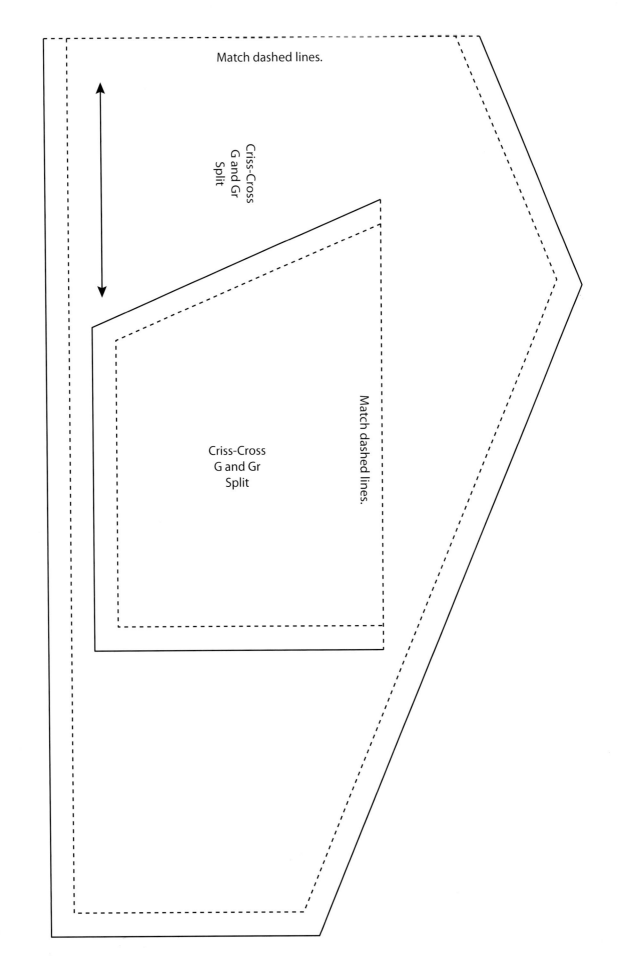

Match dashed lines.

Criss-Cross
G and Gr
Split

Criss-Cross
G and Gr
Split

Match dashed lines.

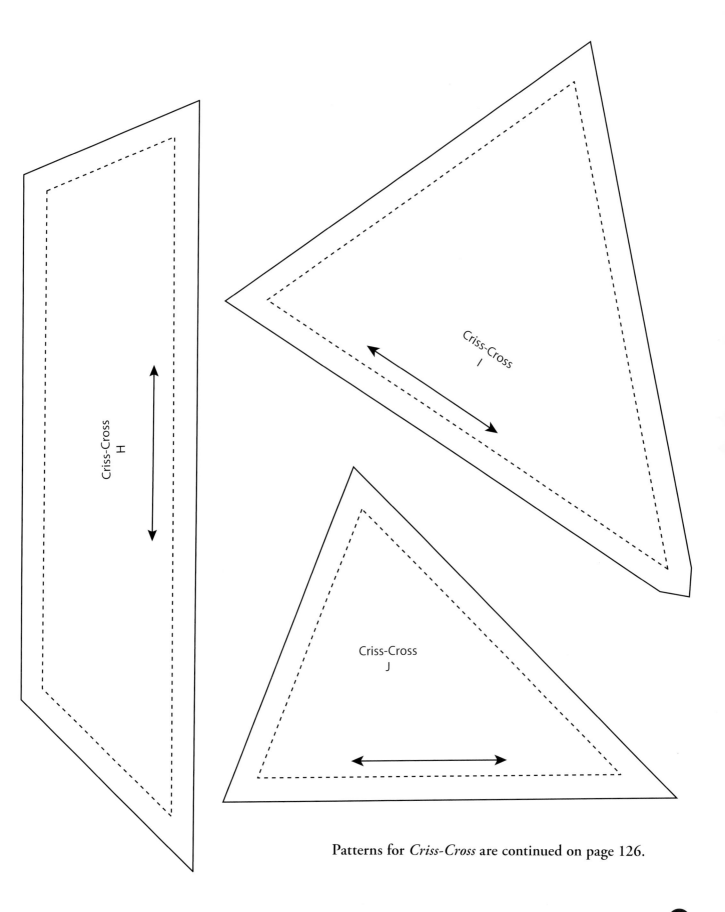

Criss-Cross
H

Criss-Cross
I

Criss-Cross
J

Patterns for *Criss-Cross* are continued on page 126.

Designed and quilted by Natalia Bonner and Kathleen Whiting;
pieced by Ashlee Woolf

Fabric shown: Mod Basics by Birch Fabrics

Eight O'Clock

FINISHED SIZE: 80″ × 90″ | **BLOCK SIZE:** 8″ × 18″

Eight O'Clock is a modern twist on a simple oval quilt block. This refreshing design is sophisticated enough to appeal to adults, but we also can imagine it in a smaller size for a toddler to play "racetrack" on with little trucks and cars. It would be the perfect gift for an 8-year-old ... or an 88-year-old! Try bold prints or pastels for completely different looks.

Materials

Yardage is based on 42″-wide fabric.

Finished size	BABY 48″ × 54″	THROW 64″ × 72″	COVERLET 80″ × 90″
DARK BLUE FABRIC	⅜ yard	¾ yard	1⅜ yards
LIGHT BLUE FABRIC	½ yard	¾ yard	1¼ yards
YELLOW FABRIC	⅜ yard	¾ yard	1¼ yards
ORANGE FABRIC	½ yard	¾ yard	1¼ yards
GREEN FABRIC	½ yard	¾ yard	1¼ yards
PINK FABRIC	½ yard	¾ yard	1¼ yards
GRAY FABRIC	2¼ yards	3½ yards	5½ yards
BACKING FABRIC	3⅛ yards	4 yards	7⅓ yards
BINDING FABRIC	½ yard	⅝ yard	¾ yard
BATTING	56″ × 62″	72″ × 80″	88″ × 98″

Cutting

Cut		BABY 18 BLOCKS	THROW 32 BLOCKS	COVERLET 50 BLOCKS
from DARK BLUE FABRIC	2¾" × 8½" strips	4	10	20
	2¾" × 4½" strips	8	20	40
	2¼" × 5" strips	4	10	20
from LIGHT BLUE FABRIC	2¾" × 8½" strips	8	10	16
	2¾" × 4½" strips	16	20	32
	2¼" × 5" strips	8	10	16
from YELLOW FABRIC	2¾" × 8½" strips	4	10	16
	2¾" × 4½" strips	8	20	32
	2¼" × 5" strips	4	10	16
from ORANGE FABRIC	2¾" × 8½" strips	6	12	16
	2¾" × 4½" strips	12	24	32
	2¼" × 5" strips	6	12	16
from GREEN FABRIC	2¾" × 8½" strips	8	10	16
	2¾" × 4½" strips	16	20	32
	2¼" × 5" strips	8	10	16
from PINK FABRIC	2¾" × 8½" strips	6	12	16
	2¾" × 4½" strips	12	24	32
	2¼" × 5" strips	6	12	16
from GRAY FABRIC	2¾" × 2¾" squares	144	256	400
	5" × 8½" strips	18	32	50
	5" × 5" squares	18	32	50

Sewing the Block

To make an Eight O'Clock block, follow these steps. Each block pairs gray with one other color. Seam allowances are ¼" unless otherwise indicated. Follow the pressing arrows.

1. Using a gray 2¾" × 2¾" square, sew a snowball corner (page 7) onto the right-hand end of a color 2¾" × 4½" strip. Make 2 (Figure A).

2. Using a gray 2¾" × 2¾" square, sew a snowball corner onto the left end of a matching color 2¾" × 4½" strip. Make 2 (Figure B).

3. Sew a unit from Step 1 to the side of the strip from Step 2, matching the gray corners as shown. Make 2 (Figure C).

4. Using 2 gray 2¾" × 2¾" squares, sew snowball corners onto both ends of a matching color 2¾" × 8½" strip. Make 2 (Figure D).

5. Sew the unit from Step 3 to the unit from Step 4. Make 2 (Figure E).

6. Sew a matching color 2¼" × 5" strip to each long side of a gray 5" × 5" square (Figure F).

7. Sew the units from Step 5 to the top and bottom of the unit from Step 6 as shown (Figure G).

8. Referring to the Eight O'Clock block diagram, sew a gray 5" × 8½" strip to the bottom of the unit from Step 7 to complete the block.

9. Repeat these steps using the different colors to make the number of blocks needed (*baby size:* 18 blocks; *throw:* 32 blocks; *coverlet:* 50 blocks).

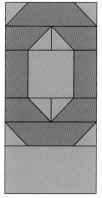

Eight O'Clock block

A.

B.

C.

D.

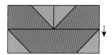

E.

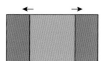

F.

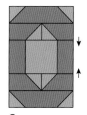

G.

Putting It All Together

Refer to the *Eight O'Clock* quilt assembly diagram to find the
quilt size you are making. Note that each block makes half of a
figure eight. When you sew the rows together, rotate the blocks in
an alternating pattern and match colors to the blocks in the row
below to achieve the figure eights. We recommend that you lay out
the quilt on a design wall or other space to plan the color placement. For the baby size, sew 3 rows of 6 blocks. For the throw,
sew 4 rows of 8 blocks. For the coverlet, sew 5 rows of 10 blocks.
Always press the seams in alternating directions from row to row.

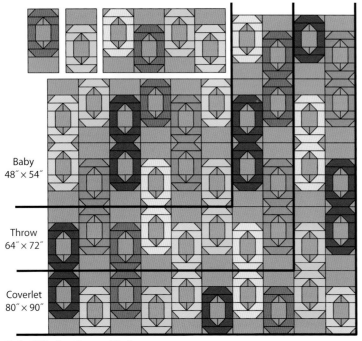

Baby
48″ × 54″

Throw
64″ × 72″

Coverlet
80″ × 90″

Eight O'Clock **quilt assembly diagram**

Finishing

Refer to Finishing the Quilt (page 11) for instructions on layering, quilting, and binding the quilt.

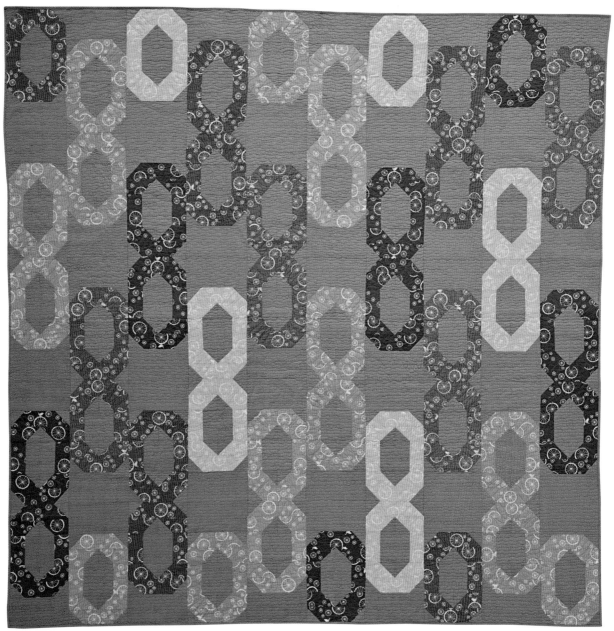

Eight O'Clock coverlet, 80″ × 90″

Designed, pieced, and quilted by Natalia Bonner and Kathleen Whiting
Fabric shown: Kona Cottons by Robert Kaufman Fabrics

E.K.G.

FINISHED SIZE: *75″ × 75″* | **BLOCK SIZE:** *15″ × 15″*

We created *E.K.G.* to be an alternative version of a classic Chevron quilt pattern. When we switched it up and added the vertical zigzags, the quilt took on a whole new look. We've made the chevrons in just two colors, but you could try making each zigzag a different color for a bright, cheerful version.

Materials

Yardage is based on 42″-wide fabric.

Finished size	BABY 45″ × 45″	THROW 60″ × 60″	COVERLET 75″ × 75″
YELLOW FABRIC	1 yard	1¼ yards	2 yards
GREEN FABRIC	1 yard	1½ yards	2¼ yards
WHITE FABRIC	2¼ yards	3⅝ yards	5¾ yards
BACKING FABRIC	3 yards	3⅞ yards	4⅝ yards
BINDING FABRIC	⅜ yard	½ yard	¾ yard
BATTING	53″ × 53″	68″ × 68″	83″ × 83″

Cutting

Cut		BABY 9 BLOCKS	THROW 16 BLOCKS	COVERLET 25 BLOCKS
from YELLOW FABRIC	3½″ × 6½″ rectangles	18	32	50
	3½″ × 3½″ squares	36	64	100
from GREEN FABRIC	3½″ × 6½″ rectangles	18	32	50
	3½″ × 3½″ squares	45	80	125
from WHITE FABRIC	3½″ × 6½″ rectangles	72	128	200
	3½″ × 3½″ squares	72	128	200

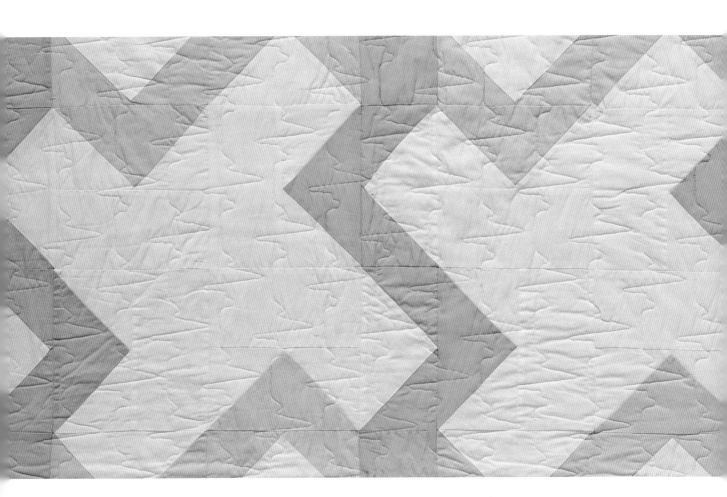

Sewing the Block

To make an E.K.G. block, follow these steps. Seam allowances are ¼″ unless otherwise indicated. Follow the pressing arrows. Refer to Flying Geese (page 8) to see additional block assembly options.

1. The instructions for this block use the Easy-Sew Method for Flying Geese units (page 9). Use 4 white 3½″ × 3½″ squares and 2 yellow 3½″ × 6½″ pieces to make 2 Flying Geese units (Figure A).

 tip First sew the right-hand white triangle, press, and then sew the left-hand white triangle.

2. Repeat Step 1, using 4 yellow 3½″ × 3½″ squares and 2 white 3½″ × 6½″ pieces to make to 2 Flying Geese units (Figure B).

3. Sew a unit from Step 1 and a unit from Step 2 together as shown. Then add a white 3½″ × 6½″ piece. Make 2 (Figure C).

4. Use 4 white 3½″ triangles and 2 green 3½″ × 6½″ pieces to make 2 Flying Geese units (Figure D).

5. Sew a white 3½″ × 6½″ piece to the top of a Flying Geese unit from Step 4. Make 2 (Figure E).

6. Sew a unit from Step 5 to a unit from Step 3 as shown. Make 2 (Figure F).

7. Use 4 green 3½″ × 3½″ squares and 2 white 3½″ × 6½″ pieces to make 2 Flying Geese units (Figure G).

8. Sew a green 3½″ × 3½″ square between the Flying Geese units from Step 7 as shown (Figure H).

9. Referring to the E.K.G. block diagram, sew the units from Step 6 to the top and bottom of the unit from Step 8 to complete the block.

10. Repeat these steps to make the number of blocks needed (*baby size:* 9 blocks; *throw:* 16 blocks; *coverlet:* 25 blocks).

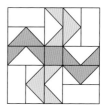

E.K.G. block

A.

B.

C.

D.

E.

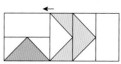

F.

G.

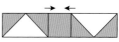

H.

Putting It All Together

Refer to the *E.K.G.* quilt assembly diagram to find the size quilt that you are making. Note the position of the blocks within the rows. For the baby size, sew 3 rows of 3 blocks. For the throw, sew 4 rows of 4 blocks. For the coverlet, sew 5 rows of 5 blocks. Always press the seams in alternating directions from row to row.

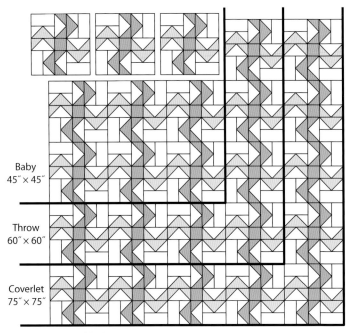

Baby
45" × 45"

Throw
60" × 60"

Coverlet
75" × 75"

E.K.G. quilt assembly diagram

Finishing

Refer to Finishing the Quilt (page 11) for instructions
on layering, quilting, and binding the quilt.

E.K.G. coverlet, 75″ × 75″

Designed, pieced, and quilted by Natalia Bonner and Kathleen Whiting
Fabrics shown: Kona Cottons by Robert Kaufman Fabrics

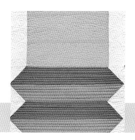

Lanterns

FINISHED SIZE: 70″ × 84″ | **BLOCK SIZE:** 14″ × 14″

Lanterns is a quick and easy quilt to put together. We've limited the palette to green solids in our quilt. You could pull prints from your stash and make each lantern a different color for an entirely different look!

Materials

Yardage is based on 42″-wide fabric.

Finished size	BABY 42″ × 42″	THROW 56″ × 56″	COVERLET 70″ × 84″
DARK GREEN FABRIC	¾ yard	1¼ yards	2¼ yards
MEDIUM GREEN FABRIC	¾ yard	1¼ yards	2¼ yards
LIGHT GREEN FABRIC	⅜ yard	⅝ yard	1⅛ yard
VERY LIGHT GREEN FABRIC	⅜ yard	⅝ yard	1⅛ yard
WHITE FABRIC	⅞ yard	1 yard	2 yards
BACKING FABRIC	2⅞ yards	4 yards	5⅛ yards
BINDING FABRIC	⅜ yard	½ yard	⅝ yard
BATTING	50″ × 50″	72″ × 72″	78″ × 92″

Cutting

tip You could use the method in Strip Piecing (page 8) to make the unit in Step 3.

Cut		BABY 9 BLOCKS	THROW 16 BLOCKS	COVERLET 30 BLOCKS
from DARK GREEN FABRIC	2½″ × 14½″ strips	18	32	60
from MEDIUM GREEN FABRIC	2½″ × 14½″ strips	18	32	60
from LIGHT GREEN FABRIC	3½″ × 10½″ strips	9	16	30
from VERY LIGHT GREEN FABRIC	3½″ × 10½″ strips	9	16	30
from WHITE FABRIC	2½″ × 6½″ strips	18	32	60
	2½″ × 2½″ squares	72	128	240

Sewing the Block

To make a Lanterns block, follow these instructions. Seam allowances are ¼" unless otherwise indicated. Follow the pressing arrows.

Lanterns block

1. Using white 2½" × 2½" squares, make snowball corners (page 7) on each end of a dark green 2½" × 14½" strip and a medium green 2½" × 14½" strip. Make 2 dark green units and 2 medium green units (Figure A).

A.

2. Sew a pair of dark green and medium green strips from Step 1 together as shown. Repeat to make a second unit (Figure B).

B.

3. Sew a light green 3½" × 10½" strip and a very light green 3½" × 10½" strip together (Figure C).

4. Sew a white 2½" × 6½" strip to each end of the strip set from Step 3 (Figure D).

C.

5. Referring to the Lanterns block diagram, sew the units from Step 2 to the unit from Step 4 to complete the block.

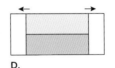

6. Repeat these steps to make the number of blocks needed (*baby size:* 9 blocks; *throw:* 16 blocks; *coverlet:* 30 blocks).

D.

Putting It All Together

Refer to the *Lanterns* quilt assembly diagram to find the quilt size you are making. For the baby size, sew 3 rows of 3 blocks. For the throw, sew 4 rows of 4 blocks. For the coverlet, sew 6 rows of 5 blocks. Note the alternating orientation of the blocks. Always press the seams in alternating directions from row to row.

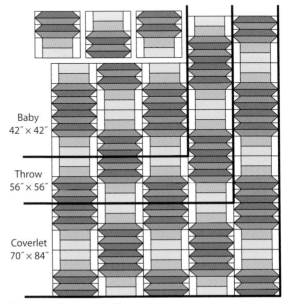

Baby
42" × 42"

Throw
56" × 56"

Coverlet
70" × 84"

***Lanterns* quilt assembly diagram**

Finishing

Refer to Finishing the Quilt (page 11) for instructions
on layering, quilting, and binding the quilt.

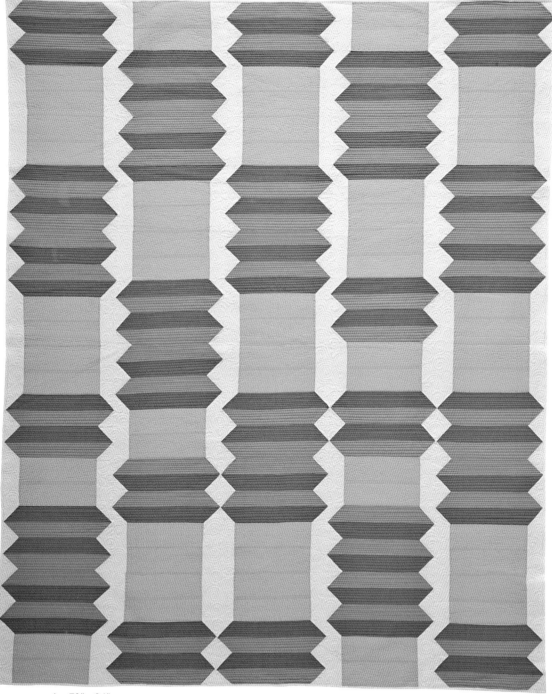

Lanterns coverlet, 70″ × 84″

Designed and quilted by Kathleen Whiting and Natalia Bonner;
pieced by Emmy Jasperson

Fabric shown: Verona by Emily Taylor Design for Riley Blake Designs

Lattice

FINISHED SIZE: 81″ × 88″ | **BLOCK SIZE:** 6¼″ × 6¼″

Red and gray latticework sparkles on this clean white background. Lattice quilts are a must-have addition to any home decor. Their graphic, repetitive lines are interesting but also evoke a sense of calm and serenity.

Don't be fooled by the diagonal lines; this quilt is put together in a straight setting and would be an ideal quilt for beginning quilters. For an alternative look, try using your scrap bag to make the latticework.

Materials

Yardage is based on 42″-wide fabric.

Finished size		BABY 50″ × 50″	THROW 69″ × 69″	COVERLET 81″ × 88″
	RED FABRIC	⅞ yard	1⅝ yards	2½ yards
	GRAY FABRIC	⅞ yard	1½ yards	2¼ yards
	WHITE FABRIC	1⅞ yards	3 yards	5⅜ yards
BACKING FABRIC		3¼ yards	4⅓ yards	7½ yards
BINDING FABRIC		½ yard	⅝ yard	¾ yard
BATTING		58″ × 58″	77″ × 77″	89″ × 96″

Cutting

Cut the squares diagonally once as indicated by the symbols.

tip You could use the method in Strip Piecing (page 8) to make the units in Step 1.

Cut			BABY 64 BLOCKS	THROW 121 BLOCKS	COVERLET 182 BLOCKS
from RED FABRIC		1¼″ × 4″ strips	128	242	364
		1¼″ × 3″ strips	128	242	364
from GRAY FABRIC		1½″ × 5¼″ strips	128	242	364
from WHITE FABRIC		4¼″ × 4¼″ squares	64 (128 triangles)	121 (242 triangles)	182 (364 triangles)
		2¼″ × 2¼″ squares	64 (128 triangles)	121 (242 triangles)	182 (364 triangles)
		2⅜″ × 5¼″ strips	64	121	182

Sewing the Block

*To make a Lattice block, follow these steps. Seam allowances are ¼"
unless otherwise indicated. Follow the pressing arrows.*

1. Sew a gray 1½" × 5¼" strip to each long side of a white
2⅜" × 5¼" strip (Figure A).

2. Sew 2 white 4¼" triangles to the strip set from Step 1 as shown
(Figure B).

3. Sew a red 1¼" × 3" strip to a short side of a 2¼" white triangle
as shown. Make 2 (Figure C).

4. Sew a red 1¼" × 4" strip to the other short side of the triangle
unit from Step 3. Make 2 (Figure D).

5. Using an acrylic ruler and rotary cutter, trim both units from
Step 4 even with the edge of the white triangle as shown
(Figure E).

6. Referring to the Lattice block diagram, sew the triangle units
from Step 5 to the unit from Step 2 to complete the block.

7. Repeat these steps to make the number of blocks needed
(*baby size:* 64 blocks; *throw:* 121 blocks; *coverlet:* 182 blocks).

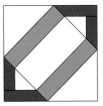

Lattice block

A.

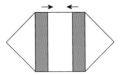

B.

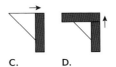

C.   D.

Cutting line

E.

Putting It All Together

Refer to the *Lattice* quilt assembly
diagram to find the size quilt you are
making. For the baby size, sew 8 rows of
8 blocks. For the throw, sew 11 rows of
11 blocks. For the coverlet, sew 14 rows
of 13 blocks. Always press the seams in
alternating directions from row to row.

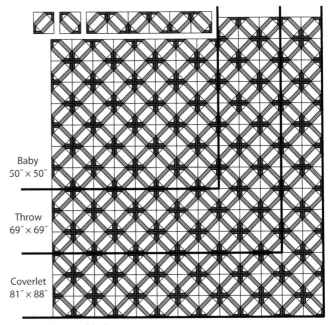

Baby
50" × 50"

Throw
69" × 69"

Coverlet
81" × 88"

Lattice quilt assembly diagram

Finishing

Refer to Finishing the Quilt (page 11) for instructions on layering, quilting, and binding the quilt.

Lattice coverlet, 81″ × 88″

Designed, pieced, and quilted by Natalia Bonner and Kathleen Whiting
Fabric shown: Bella Solids by Moda Fabrics

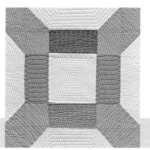

Mellow

FINISHED SIZE: 90″ × 90″ | **BLOCK SIZE:** 18″ × 18″

Big, boxy pieces and a fresh color palette bring a contemporary flair to this easy-to-make quilt. While adults may think that *Mellow* has a modern-art edge that makes it a perfect wall quilt, children may see roadways and intersections in the graphic design and beg to put it on the floor for playtime.

Materials

Yardage is based on 42″-wide fabric.

Finished size	BABY 54″ × 54″	THROW 72″ × 72″	COVERLET 90″ × 90″
YELLOW-GREEN FABRIC	1¼ yards	2¼ yards	3⅜ yards
GRAY FABRIC	1 yard	1⅜ yards	2 yards
WHITE FABRIC	1¾ yards	2¾ yards	3¾ yards
BACKING FABRIC	3½ yards	4½ yards	8¼ yards
BINDING FABRIC	½ yard	⅝ yard	¾ yard
BATTING	62″ × 62″	80″ × 80″	98″ × 98″

Cutting

 tip You could use the method in Strip Piecing (page 8) to make the units in Step 4.

Cut		BABY 9 BLOCKS	THROW 16 BLOCKS	COVERLET 25 BLOCKS
from YELLOW-GREEN FABRIC	3½″ × 3½″ squares	72	128	200
	3⅞″ × 3⅞″ squares	36	64	100
from GRAY FABRIC	3½″ × 6½″ strips	36	64	100
from WHITE FABRIC	3½″ × 6½″ strips	36	64	100
	3⅞″ × 3⅞″ squares	36	64	100
	6½″ × 6½″ squares	9	16	25

Sewing the Block

*To make a Mellow block, follow these steps. Seam allowances are ¼"
unless otherwise indicated. Follow the pressing arrows.*

1. Use a white 3⅞" × 3⅞" square and a yellow-green 3⅞" × 3⅞"
square to make 2 half-square triangles, using the No-Waste
Method (page 8). Repeat to make a total of 8 half-square
triangles (Figure A).

2. Sew a row containing 2 yellow-green 3½" × 3½" squares,
2 half-square triangles, and a white 3½" × 6½" strip as shown.
Make 2 rows (Figure B).

3. Sew a row containing 2 half-square triangles, 2 yellow-green
3½" × 3½" squares, and a gray 3½" × 6½" strip as shown.
Make 2 rows (Figure C).

4. Sew a row containing 2 white 3½" × 6½" strips, 2 gray
3½" × 6½" strips, and a white 6½" × 6½" square as shown
(Figure D).

5. Referring to the Mellow block diagram, sew the rows from
Steps 2–4 together to complete the block.

6. Repeat these steps to make the number of blocks needed
(*baby size:* 9 blocks; *throw:* 16 blocks; *coverlet:* 25 blocks).

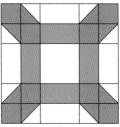

Mellow block

A.

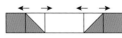

B.

C.

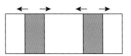

D.

Putting It All Together

Refer to the *Mellow* quilt assembly diagram
to find the size quilt you are making. For
the baby size, sew 3 rows of 3 blocks. For
the throw, sew 4 rows of 4 blocks. For the
coverlet, sew 5 rows of 5 blocks. Always
press the seams in alternating directions
from row to row.

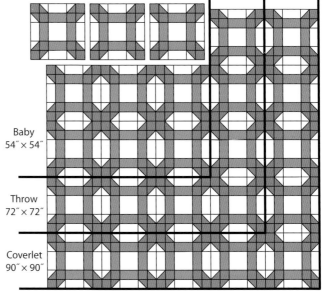

Baby
54" × 54"

Throw
72" × 72"

Coverlet
90" × 90"

Mellow **quilt assembly diagram**

Finishing

Refer to Finishing the Quilt (page 11) for instructions on layering, quilting, and binding the quilt.

Mellow coverlet, 90″ × 90″

Designed, pieced, and quilted by Natalia Bonner and Kathleen Whiting
Fabric shown: Kona Cottons by Robert Kaufman Fabrics

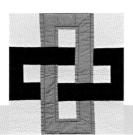

Paper Clips

FINISHED SIZE: 84″ × 84″ | **BLOCK SIZE:** 14″ × 14″

Quilters can find inspiration from anywhere, as we can attest with our ode to the paper clip. These interlocking open rectangles have a very contemporary flair in just two colors on a white background. For a lively alternative, try using scraps to make each paper clip a different color.

Materials

Yardage is based on 42″-wide fabric.

Finished size		BABY 42″ × 42″	THROW 70″ × 70″	COVERLET 84″ × 84″
	PURPLE FABRIC	⅞ yard	1⅝ yards	2⅝ yards
	GRAY FABRIC	⅞ yard	2¼ yards	2¾ yards
	WHITE FABRIC	1 yard	2⅜ yards	3¼ yards
BACKING FABRIC		2⅞ yards	4½ yards	7⅞ yards
BINDING FABRIC		⅜ yard	⅝ yard	¾ yard
BATTING		50″ × 50″	78″ × 78″	92″ × 92″

Cutting

 tip You could use the method in Strip Piecing (page 8) to make the units in Steps 1 and 5.

Cut		BABY 9 BLOCKS	THROW 25 BLOCKS	COVERLET 36 BLOCKS
from PURPLE FABRIC	2½″ × 4½″ strips	36	100	144
	2½″ × 2½″ squares	54	150	216
from GRAY FABRIC	2½″ × 8½″ strips	18	50	72
	2½″ × 4½″ strips	18	50	72
	2½″ × 2½″ squares	18	50	72
from WHITE FABRIC	4½″ × 4½″ squares	36	100	144
	2½″ × 2½″ squares	45	125	180

Sewing the Block

To make a Paper Clips block, follow these steps. Seam allowances are ¼" unless otherwise indicated. Follow the pressing arrows.

1. Sew a white 2½" × 2½" square and a purple 2½" × 2½" square together. Make 4 (Figure A).

2. Sew a purple 2½" × 4½" strip to opposite sides of a strip set from Step 1 as shown. Make 2 (Figure B).

3. Sew 2 white 4½" × 4½" squares to a unit from Step 2 as shown. Make 2 rows (Figure C).

4. Sew 2 units from Step 1 together and add a white 2½" × 2½" square to the purple end (Figure D).

5. Add a gray 2½" × 2½" square to each end of the row from Step 4 as shown (Figure E).

6. Sew a gray 2½" × 8½" strip, a purple 2½" × 2½" square, and a gray 2½" × 4½" strip together as shown. Make 2 rows (Figure F).

7. Referring to the Paper Clips block diagram, sew the rows from Steps 3, 5, and 6 together as shown to complete the block.

8. Repeat these steps to make the number of blocks needed (*baby size:* 9 blocks; *throw:* 25 blocks; *coverlet:* 36 blocks).

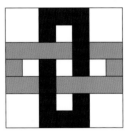

Paper Clips block

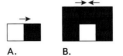

A.   **B.**

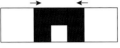

C.

D.

E.

F.

Putting It All Together

Refer to the *Paper Clips* quilt assembly diagram to find the size quilt you are making. For the baby size, sew 3 rows of 3 blocks. For the throw, sew 5 rows of 5 blocks. For the coverlet, sew 6 rows of 6 blocks. Rotate every other block in the rows. Always press the seams in alternating directions from row to row.

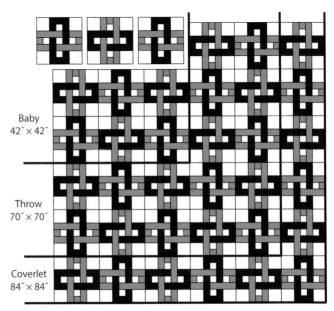

Baby
42" × 42"

Throw
70" × 70"

Coverlet
84" × 84"

***Paper Clips* quilt assembly diagram**

Finishing

Refer to Finishing the Quilt (page 11) for instructions on layering, quilting, and binding the quilt.

Paper Clips **coverlet, 84″ × 84″**

Designed, pieced, and quilted by Natalia Bonner and Kathleen Whiting
Fabric shown: Summersville by Lucie Summers for Moda Fabrics

Rotating Snowballs

FINISHED SIZE: 75″ × 90″ **| BLOCK SIZE:** 7½″ × 7½″

A wide stripe in the center of each snowball gives a fresh look to this traditional block. Rotating the direction of the stripe in every other block adds movement to the design.

A calm, cool quilt in blue and white, *Rotating Snowballs* could be a cheerful holiday quilt with the balls and stripes made in reds and greens. Made in scraps, this quilt would be a quick and easy project for a block exchange.

Materials

Yardage is based on 42″-wide fabric.

Finished size	BABY 45″ × 45″	THROW 60″ × 60″	COVERLET 75″ × 90″
SOLID BLUE FABRIC	1⅛ yards	2 yards	3¼ yards
MEDIUM BLUE FABRIC	1 yard	1½ yards	2⅝ yards
WHITE FABRIC	1⅝ yards	2¾ yards	4¾ yards
BACKING FABRIC	3 yards	4 yards	5½ yards
BINDING FABRIC	½ yard	⅝ yard	¾ yard
BATTING	53″ × 53″	68″ × 68″	83″ × 98″

Cutting

 tip You could use the method in Strip Piecing (page 8) to make the units in Step 1.

Cut		BABY 36 BLOCKS	THROW 64 BLOCKS	COVERLET 120 BLOCKS
from DARK BLUE FABRIC	3″ × 3″ squares	144	256	480
from MEDIUM BLUE FABRIC	3″ × 8″ strips	36	64	120
from WHITE FABRIC	3″ × 8″ strips	72	128	240

Sewing the Block

To make a Rotating Snowballs block, follow these steps. Seam allowances are ¼" unless otherwise indicated. Follow the pressing arrows.

1. Sew a white 3" × 8" strip to each long side of a medium blue 3" × 8" strip (Figure A).

2. Referring to the Rotating Snowballs block diagram, use a dark blue 3" × 3" square to make a snowball corner (page 7) on each corner of the unit from Step 1 to complete the block.

3. Repeat these steps to make the number of blocks needed (*baby size:* 36 blocks; *throw:* 64 blocks; *coverlet:* 120 blocks).

Putting It All Together

Refer to the *Rotating Snowballs* quilt assembly diagram to find the size quilt that you are making. For the baby size, sew 6 rows of 6 blocks. For the throw, sew 8 rows of 8 blocks. For the coverlet, sew 12 rows of 10 blocks. Rotate the direction of the center stripe in every other block. Always press the seams in alternating directions from row to row.

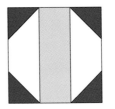

Rotating Snowballs block

A.

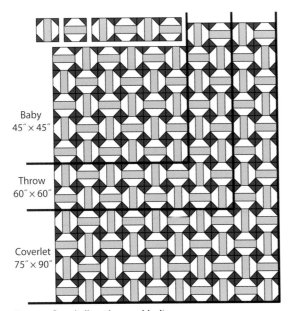

Baby
45" × 45"

Throw
60" × 60"

Coverlet
75" × 90"

Rotating Snowballs **quilt assembly diagram**

Finishing

Refer to Finishing the Quilt (page 11) for instructions on layering, quilting, and binding the quilt.

Rotating Snowballs coverlet, 75″ × 90″

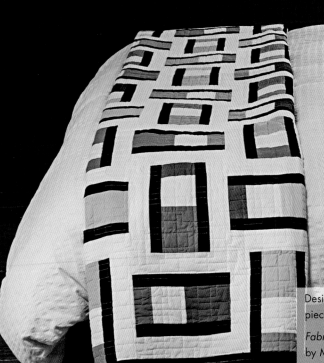

Designed and quilted by Natalia Bonner and Kathleen Whiting; pieced by Emmy Jasperson

Fabrics shown: Kona Cottons by Robert Kaufman Fabrics, Bella Solids by Moda Fabrics, and Cotton Couture by Michael Miller Fabrics

Squared Scraps

FINISHED SIZE: 81″ × 99″ | **BLOCK SIZE:** 9″ × 9″

What a great stash buster this quilt is! *Squared Scraps* is a simple yet very effective use of solid or print scraps. Or, mix it up and use solids and prints in the same quilt. Head to your stash, pull out a pile of scraps, and have fun!

Materials

Yardage is based on 42″-wide fabric.

Finished size	BABY 36″ × 54″	THROW 72″ × 72″	COVERLET 81″ × 99″
ASSORTED PRINTS/SOLIDS	1 yard	1¾ yards	2½ yards
BLACK FABRIC	⅞ yard	1⅝ yards	2½ yards
WHITE FABRIC	1⅜ yards	3⅛ yards	4½ yards
BACKING FABRIC	1¾ yards	4½ yards	7½ yards
BINDING FABRIC	⅜ yard	⅝ yard	¾ yard
BATTING	42″ × 62″	80″ × 80″	89″ × 107″

Cutting

Cut		BABY 24 BLOCKS	THROW 64 BLOCKS	COVERLET 99 BLOCKS
from ASSORTED PRINTS/SOLIDS	4½″ × 3½″ pieces	24	64	99
	2½″ × 3½″ pieces	24	64	99
from WHITE FABRIC	2½″ × 9½″ strips	48	128	198
	3½″ × 3½″ squares	24	64	99
from BLACK FABRIC	1½″ × 9½″ strips	48	128	198

Sewing the Block

To make a Squared Scraps block, follow these steps. Seam allowances are ¼" unless otherwise indicated. Follow the pressing arrows.

Squared Scraps block

1. Sew a color 2½" × 3½" strip and a different color 4½" × 3½" strip to opposite sides of a white 3½" × 3½" square as shown (Figure A).

2. Sew black 1½" × 9½" strips to the unit from Step 1 as shown (Figure B).

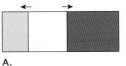

A.

3. Referring to the Squared Scraps block diagram, sew a white 2½" × 9½" strip to both long sides of the unit from Step 2 to complete the block.

4. Repeat these steps to make the number of blocks needed (*baby size:* 24 blocks; *throw:* 64 blocks; *coverlet:* 99 blocks).

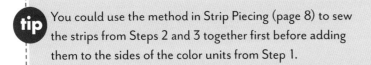

B.

> **tip** You could use the method in Strip Piecing (page 8) to sew the strips from Steps 2 and 3 together first before adding them to the sides of the color units from Step 1.

Putting It All Together

Refer to the *Squared Scraps* quilt assembly diagram to find the size quilt you are making. Note the block placement and rotate the blocks within the rows. For the baby size, sew 6 rows of 4 blocks. For the throw, sew 8 rows of 8 blocks. For the coverlet, sew 11 rows of 9 blocks. Alternate the direction and color of every other block. Always press the seams in alternating directions from row to row.

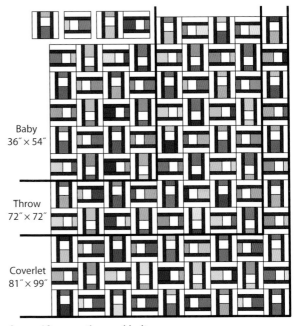

Baby
36" × 54"

Throw
72" × 72"

Coverlet
81" × 99"

Squared Scraps quilt assembly diagram

Finishing

Refer to Finishing the Quilt (page 11) for instructions
on layering, quilting, and binding the quilt.

Squared Scraps coverlet, 81″ × 99″

Designed, pieced, and quilted by Natalia Bonner and Kathleen Whiting
Fabric shown: Cotton Couture by Michael Miller Fabrics

Twisty

FINISHED SIZE: 80″ × 80″ | **BLOCK SIZE:** 16″ × 16″

Large, squared-off spirals sing in this graphic quilt. To add interest, we created an ombré look with each row in a different shade of purple. *Twisty* is a fun quilt that would be appealing in a wide array of fabrics.

Materials

Yardage is based on 42"-wide fabric.

Finished size	BABY 48" × 48"	THROW 64" × 64"	COVERLET 80" × 80"
PURPLE 1 FABRIC	½ yard	¾ yard	⅞ yard
PURPLE 2 FABRIC	½ yard	¾ yard	⅞ yard
PURPLE 3 FABRIC	½ yard	¾ yard	⅞ yard
PURPLE 4 FABRIC		¾ yard	⅞ yard
PURPLE 5 FABRIC			⅞ yard
WHITE FABRIC	1½ yards	2½ yards	3½ yards
BACKING FABRIC	3⅛ yards	4 yards	7⅓ yards
BINDING FABRIC	½ yard	½ yard	¾ yard
BATTING	56" × 56"	72" × 72"	88" × 88"

Cutting

Cut the longest strips first. Then cut the shorter pieces from the leftover strips.

> **tip** You could use the method in Strip Piecing (page 8) to make the unit in Step 3.

Cut		BABY 9 BLOCKS	THROW 16 BLOCKS	COVERLET 25 BLOCKS
from PURPLE FABRICS		PURPLE 1 PURPLE 2 PURPLE 3	PURPLE 1 PURPLE 2 PURPLE 3 PURPLE 4	PURPLE 1 PURPLE 2 PURPLE 3 PURPLE 4 PURPLE 5
	2½″ × 16½″ strips	3 of each	4 of each	5 of each
	2½″ × 14½″ strips	3 of each	4 of each	5 of each
	2½″ × 12½″ strips	3 of each	4 of each	5 of each
	2½″ × 10½″ strips	3 of each	4 of each	5 of each
	2½″ × 8½″ strips	3 of each	4 of each	5 of each
	2½″ × 6½″ strips	3 of each	4 of each	5 of each
	2½″ × 4½″ strips	3 of each	4 of each	5 of each
	2½″ × 2½″ squares	3 of each	4 of each	5 of each
from WHITE FABRIC	2½″ × 14½″ strips	9 of each	16 of each	25 of each
	2½″ × 12½″ strips	9 of each	16 of each	25 of each
	2½″ × 10½″ strips	9 of each	16 of each	25 of each
	2½″ × 8½″ strips	9 of each	16 of each	25 of each
	2½″ × 6½″ strips	9 of each	16 of each	25 of each
	2½″ × 4½″ strips	9 of each	16 of each	25 of each
	2½″ × 2½″ squares	9 of each	16 of each	25 of each

Sewing the Block

To make a Twisty block of a single color, follow these steps. Seam allowances are ¼" unless otherwise indicated. Follow the pressing arrows.

1. Sew a purple 2½" × 2½" square and a white 2½" × 2½" square together (Figure A).

2. Sew a matching purple 2½" × 4½" strip and a white 2½" × 4½" strip to each side of the strip set from Step 1 as shown (Figure B).

3. Sew a white 2½" × 6½" strip to the bottom of the unit (Figure C).

4. Sew a matching purple 2½" × 6½" strip to the right-hand side of the unit (Figure D).

5. Sew a matching purple 2½" × 8½" strip to the top of the unit (Figure E).

6. Sew a white 2½" × 8½" strip to the left side of the unit (Figure F).

7. Sew a matching purple 2½" × 10½" strip to the bottom of the unit (Figure G).

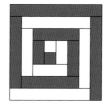

Twisty block

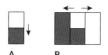

A. B.

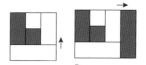

C. D.

E. F.

G.

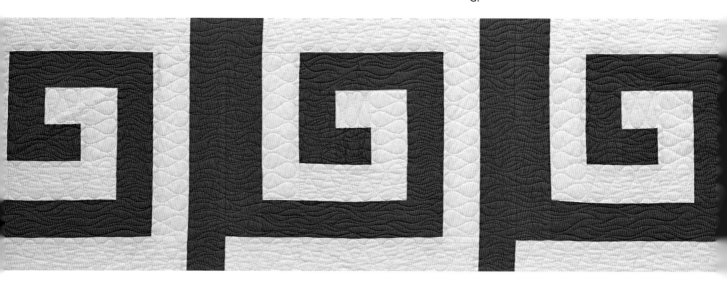

8. Sew a white 2½″ × 10½″ strip to the right side of the unit (Figure H).

9. Sew a white 2½″ × 12½″ strip to the top of the unit (Figure I).

10. Sew a matching purple 2½″ × 12½″ strip to the left side of the unit (Figure J).

11. Sew a white 2½″ × 14½″ strip to the bottom of the unit (Figure K).

12. Sew a matching purple 2½″ × 14½″ strip to the right side of the unit (Figure L).

13. Referring to the Twisty block diagram (page 107), sew a matching purple 2½″ × 16½″ strip to the top of the unit to complete the block.

14. Repeat these steps to make the number of blocks needed (*baby size:* 3 blocks of each purple; *throw:* 4 blocks of each purple; *coverlet:* 5 blocks of each purple).

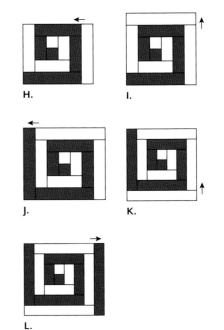

Putting It All Together

Refer to the *Twisty* quilt assembly diagram to find the size quilt that you are making. Make each row a different shade of purple and arrange the rows from light to dark, positioning the blocks as shown. For the baby size, sew 3 rows of 3 blocks. For the throw, sew 4 rows of 4 blocks. For the coverlet, sew 5 rows of 5 blocks. Always press the seams in alternating directions from row to row.

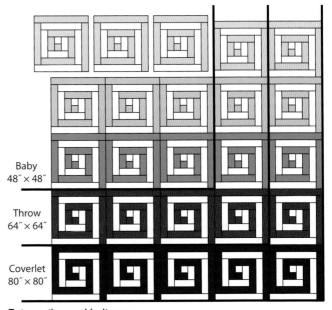

Baby
48″ × 48″

Throw
64″ × 64″

Coverlet
80″ × 80″

Twisty quilt assembly diagram

Finishing

Refer to Finishing the Quilt (page 11) for instructions
on layering, quilting, and binding the quilt.

Twisty coverlet, 80″ × 80″

Designed, pieced, and quilted by Natalia Bonner and Kathleen Whiting
Fabrics shown: Birds and Berries by Lauren and Jessi Jung for Moda Fabrics

Wacky Flowers

FINISHED SIZE: *75″ × 90″* **I BLOCK SIZE:** *7½″ × 7½″*

These funky, simple flowers make us smile! *Wacky Flowers* contains just four pieces per block, so this quilt goes together quickly.

Materials

Yardage is based on 42″-wide fabric.

Finished size	BABY 45″ × 45″	THROW 60″ × 60″	COVERLET 75″ × 90″
PURPLE FABRIC	¾ yard	1⅛ yards	2 yards
ORANGE FABRIC	⅜ yard	½ yard	⅞ yard
WHITE FABRIC	2⅛ yards	3⅝ yards	6¼ yards
BACKING FABRIC	3 yards	3¾ yards	5½ yards
BINDING FABRIC	½ yard	⅝ yard	¾ yard
BATTING	53″ × 53″	68″ × 68″	83″ × 98″

Cutting

Copy the Wacky Flowers *patterns A and B (pages 113 and 114) at 100%. Refer to Template Piecing (page 10) for instructions on cutting the indicated pieces. Cut the squares diagonally once as indicated by the symbol.*

Cut		BABY 36 BLOCKS	THROW 64 BLOCKS	COVERLET 120 BLOCKS
from PURPLE FABRIC	Templates A and Ar	36 of each	64 of each	120 of each
from ORANGE FABRIC	3⅜" × 3⅜" squares	18 (36 triangles)	32 (64 triangles)	60 (120 triangles)
from WHITE FABRIC	Template B	36	64	120

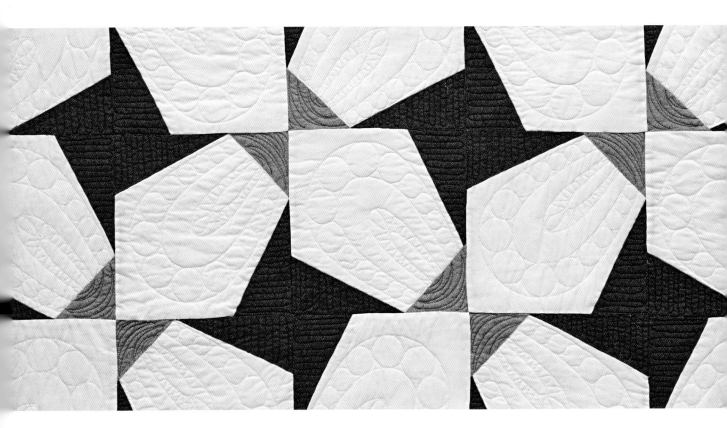

Sewing the Block

To make a Wacky Flowers block, follow these steps. Refer to Template Piecing (page 10) for tips on using this method. Seam allowances are ¼" unless otherwise indicated. Follow the pressing arrows.

1. Make an A/B/Ar unit (Figure A).

2. Referring to the Wacky Flowers block diagram, sew an orange triangle as the missing corner to the block as shown.

3. Repeat these steps to make the number of blocks needed (*baby size:* 36 blocks; *throw:* 64 blocks; *coverlet:* 120 blocks).

Wacky Flowers block

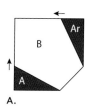

A.

Putting It All Together

Refer to the *Wacky Flowers* quilt assembly diagram to find the size quilt you are making. For the baby size, sew 6 rows of 6 blocks. For the throw, sew 8 rows of 8 blocks. For the coverlet, sew 12 rows of 10 blocks. Rotate every other block in the rows to create a sense of movement. Always press the seams in alternating directions from row to row.

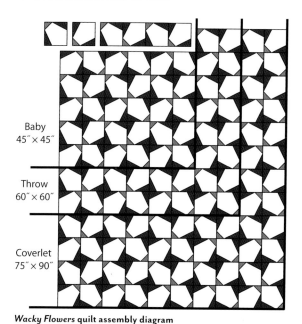

Baby
45" × 45"

Throw
60" × 60"

Coverlet
75" × 90"

***Wacky Flowers* quilt assembly diagram**

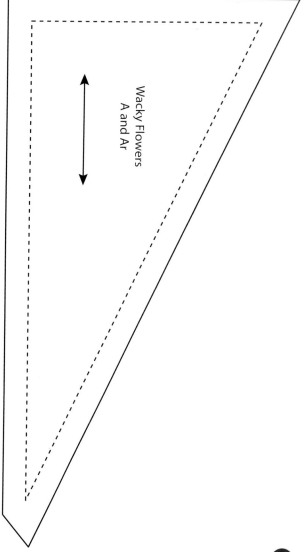

Wacky Flowers
A and Ar

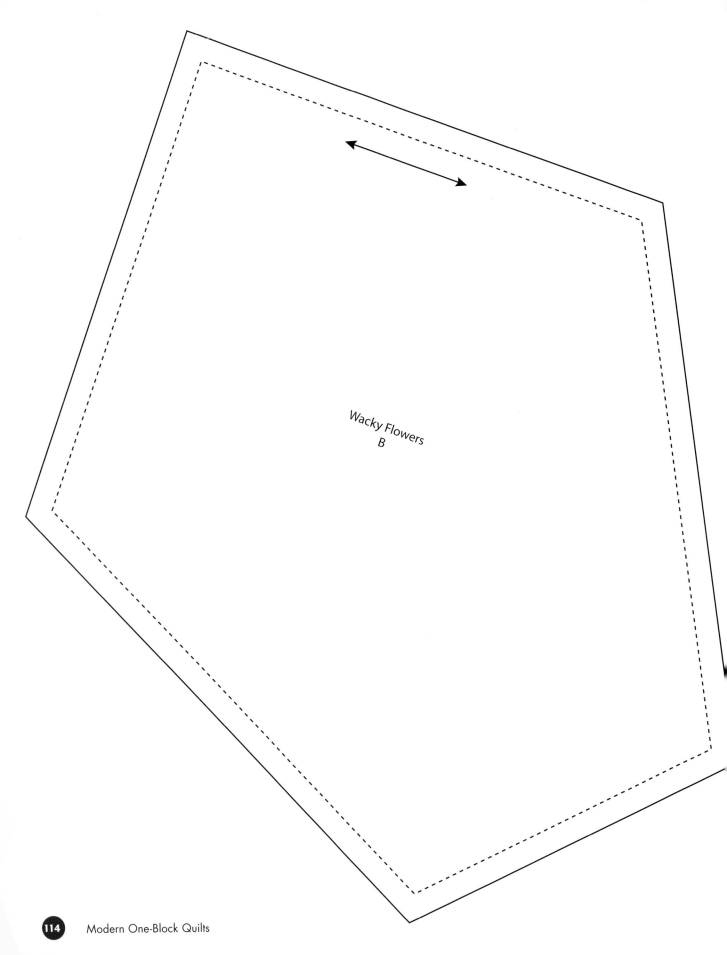

Wacky Flowers
B

Finishing

Refer to Finishing the Quilt (page 11) for instructions
on layering, quilting, and binding the quilt.

Wacky Flowers **coverlet, 75″ × 90″**

Designed, pieced, and quilted by Natalia Bonner and Kathleen Whiting
Fabric shown: Bella Solids by Moda Fabrics

Weaving

FINISHED SIZE: 90″ × 90″ **|** **BLOCK SIZE:** 18″ × 18″

A classic plaid design in just three colors comes to life in this cheerful quilt. The quilt appears to be set on point but it's actually put together in an easy straight setting.

Materials

Yardage is based on 42"-wide fabric.

Finished size	BABY 36" × 36"	THROW 72" × 72"	COVERLET 90" × 90"
YELLOW FABRIC	½ yard	1¼ yards	1⅞ yards
ORANGE FABRIC	1¼ yards	2¼ yards	3⅛ yards
WHITE FABRIC	1¼ yards	3¼ yards	5 yards
BACKING FABRIC	2½ yards	4½ yards	8¼ yards
BINDING FABRIC	½ yard	⅝ yard	¾ yard
BATTING	44" × 44"	80" × 80"	98" × 98"

Cutting

Cut the longest strips first. Then cut the shorter strips from the leftover strips.

Cut the squares diagonally twice as indicated by the symbol.

tip You could use the method in Strip Piecing (page 8) to make the strip sets in Step 1.

Cut		BABY 4 BLOCKS	THROW 16 BLOCKS	COVERLET 25 BLOCKS
from **YELLOW** **FABRIC**	1½″ × 28″ strips	4	16	25
	1½″ × 9″ strips	16	64	100
from **ORANGE** **FABRIC**	2⅝″ × 7¾″ strips	16	64	100
	2⅝″ × 11″ strips	8	32	50
from **WHITE** **FABRIC**	5¼″ × 5¼″ squares	16	64	100
	8″ × 8″ squares	8 (32 triangles)	32 (128 triangles)	50 (200 triangles)

Sewing the Block

To make a Weaving block, follow these steps. Seam allowances are ¼″ unless otherwise indicated. Follow the pressing arrows.

1. Sew a white 5¼″ × 5¼″ square onto each side of a yellow 1½″ × 5¼″ strip. Make 2 (Figure A).

2. Sew an orange 2⅝″ × 11″ strip to the bottom of the strip set from Step 1. Make 2 (Figure B).

3. Sew an orange 2⅝″ × 7¾″ strip to each side of the units from Step 2 as shown. Make 2 (Figure C).

4. Sew a white triangle to the orange strips on the unit from Step 3 as shown. Then, using a ruler and rotary cutter, trim the orange strips following the angle of the triangles as shown (Figure D).

5. Sew a white triangle to each long side of the yellow 1½″ × 9″ strip. Then using a ruler and a rotary cutter, trim the end of the yellow strip, following the angles of the triangles as shown. Make 2 (Figure E).

6. Sew a unit from Step 5 to a unit from Step 4. Make 2 (Figure F).

7. Match the center of the unit from Step 6 to the center of a yellow 1½″ × 28″ strip. Sew together. Then trim the ends of the yellow strip, following the angles of the white triangles as you did before (Figure G).

8. Referring to the Weaving block diagram, sew the remaining unit from Step 6 to the unit from Step 7 to complete the block, matching the centers and trimming the ends of the yellow strip as in Step 7.

9. Repeat these steps to make the number of blocks needed (*baby size:* 4 blocks; *throw:* 16 blocks; *coverlet:* 25 blocks).

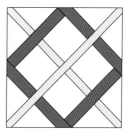

Weaving block

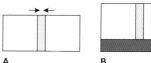

A.   B.

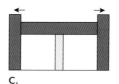

C.

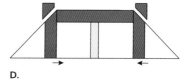

D.

E.

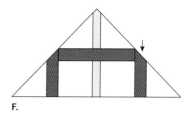

F.

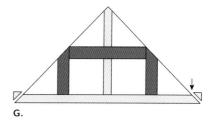

G.

Putting It All Together

Refer to the *Weaving* quilt assembly diagram to find the size quilt you are making. For the baby size, sew 2 rows of 2 blocks. For the throw, sew 4 rows of 4 blocks. For the coverlet, sew 5 rows of 5 blocks. Always press the seams in alternating directions from row to row.

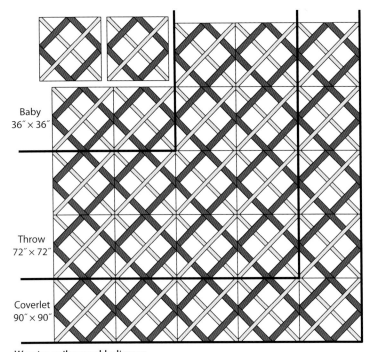

Baby
36″ × 36″

Throw
72″ × 72″

Coverlet
90″ × 90″

Weaving quilt assembly diagram

Finishing

Refer to Finishing the Quilt (page 11) for instructions on layering, quilting, and binding the quilt.

Weaving coverlet, 90″ × 90″

Designed and quilted by Natalia Bonner and Kathleen Whiting;
pieced by Emmy Jasperson

Fabric shown: Bella by Lotta Jansdotter for Windham Fabrics

Wiggling

FINISHED SIZE: *66" × 77"* | **BLOCK SIZE:** *11" × 11"*

 tip Moda Charm Packs contain 40 squares 5" × 5", or about 1 yard of fabric.

Wiggling is a funky quilt that is perfect for charm packs or 5" × 5" squares. Use just one charm pack for a baby quilt or multiple charm packs to create a coverlet in a short amount of time.

Materials

Yardage is based on 42"-wide fabric.

Finished size	BABY 44" × 44"	THROW 55" × 55"	COVERLET 66" × 77"
BLUE FABRIC	1¼ yards	1⅝ yards	2⅝ yards
ASSORTED COLORS OF PRINTS	1½ yards	2⅛ yards	3¾ yards
BACKING FABRIC	3 yards	3½ yards	4¾ yards
BINDING FABRIC	⅜ yard	½ yard	⅝ yard
BATTING	52" × 52"	63" × 63"	74" × 85"

Cutting

Cut		BABY 16 BLOCKS	THROW 25 BLOCKS	COVERLET 42 BLOCKS
from BLUE FABRIC	1½" × 6" strips	64	100	168
	1½" × 5" strips	64	100	168
from ASSORTED COLORS OF PRINTS	5" × 5" squares	64	100	168

Sewing the Block

*To make a Wiggling block, follow these steps. Seam allowances are ¼"
unless otherwise indicated. Follow the pressing arrows.*

Wiggling block

> **tip** You could use the method in Strip Piecing (page 8) to make
> the units in Step 1.

1. Sew a blue 1½" × 5" strip to a print 5" × 5" square. Make 4,
using a variety of colored squares (Figure A).

A.

2. Sew a blue 1½" × 6" strip to the left side of the unit from Step 1
as shown. Make 4 (Figure B).

B.

3. Sew 2 of the units from Step 2 together as shown. Make 2
(Figure C).

4. Referring to the Wiggling block diagram, sew the units from
Step 3 together to complete the block.

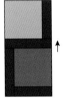

5. Repeat these steps to make the number of blocks needed
(*baby size:* 16 blocks; *throw:* 25 blocks; *coverlet:* 42 blocks).

C.

Putting It All Together

Refer to the *Wiggling* quilt assembly diagram to
find the size quilt that you are making. For the
baby size, sew 4 rows of 4 blocks. For the throw,
sew 5 rows of 5 blocks. For the coverlet, sew
7 rows of 6 blocks. Always press the seams in
alternating directions from row to row.

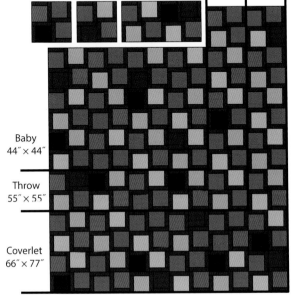

Baby
44" × 44"

Throw
55" × 55"

Coverlet
66" × 77"

***Wiggling* quilt assembly diagram**

Finishing

Refer to Finishing the Quilt (page 11) for instructions on layering, quilting, and binding the quilt.

Wiggling coverlet, 66″ × 77″

Criss-Cross project is on page 58. Patterns for *Criss-Cross* are continued from pages 64 to 67.

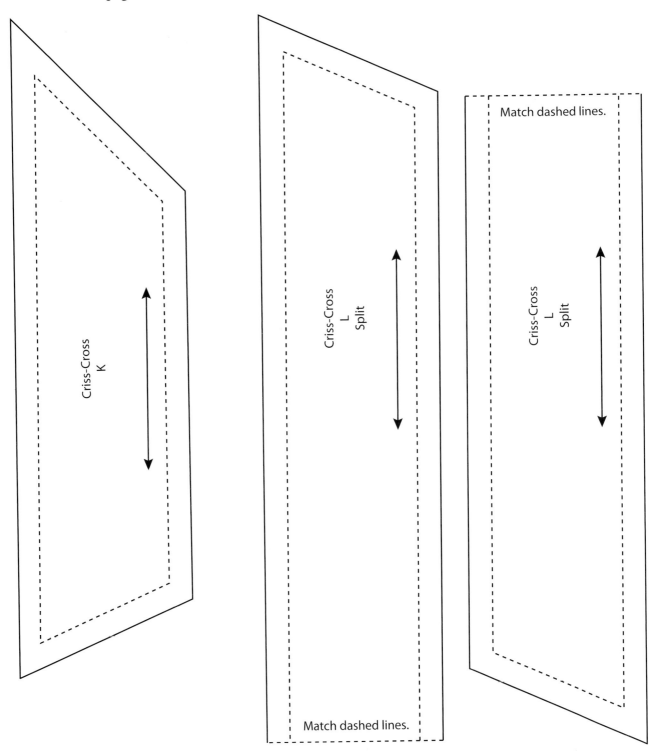

About the Authors

Photo by Whitnee North

NATALIA WHITING BONNER has enjoyed piecing quilt tops for more than twenty years. She learned how to quilt on her conventional home machine. She felt good about it, but decided that if she really wanted to take her quilting to the next level, she needed to invest in a longarm machine. In 2007, when she was pregnant with her daughter, she got the crazy idea to quit her job as a dental assistant and become a longarm quilter. She spent a day at a longarm dealer's shop and walked out after purchasing a Gammill machine. Natalia's passion for quilting and being creative has grown each day since.

Natalia has won numerous awards for her work and has been featured on the Moda Bake Shop website; in *Quiltmaker*, *Fons & Porter's Love of Quilting*, and *American Patchwork & Quilting* magazines; in her book *Beginner's Guide to Free-Motion Quilting*; and as a contributor in the books *Fresh Fabric Treats*, *Modern Blocks*, and *Sweet Celebrations with the Moda Bake Shop Chefs* (all books by C&T Publishing). Visit her blog at pieceandquilt.com.

Photo by Whitnee North

KATHLEEN JASPERSON WHITING has been sewing for as long as she can remember. Her mother and grandmother always had a quilting project going on, so naturally quilting became part of her life.

Kathleen is from Boise, Idaho, and has lived the past 35 years in a small town in the Utah mountains where she raised 5 children and now is grandma to 5 granddaughters and a grandson. Sewing, quilting, designing, and decorating are her passions.

In 2010 Kathleen was named the first *McCall's Quilting* Quilt Design Star. She has won numerous awards for her quilts, and her designs have been published in several magazines—*American Patchwork & Quilting*, *Fons & Porter's Love of Quilting*, *Quiltmaker*, and *McCall's Quilting*.

Also by Natalia Bonner:

stashBOOKS

fabric arts for a handmade lifestyle

If you're craving beautiful authenticity in a time of mass-production...Stash Books is for you. Stash Books is a line of how-to books celebrating fabric arts for a handmade lifestyle. Backed by C&T Publishing's solid reputation for quality, Stash Books will inspire you with contemporary designs, clear and simple instructions, and engaging photography.

www.stashbooks.com